2022

To: Dr. Jacksson

Thank you for your review + endorsement. God bless you! ☺

LEADERSHIP
WITH A SERVANT'S HEART

LEADING IN YOUR
WORKPLACE

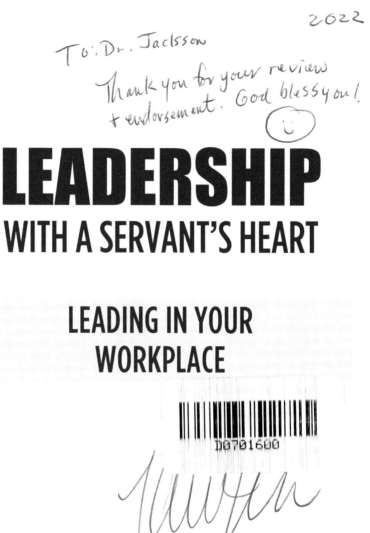

D0701600

LEADERSHIP

WITH A SERVANT'S HEART

LEADING IN YOUR WORKPLACE

KEVIN WAYNE JOHNSON

Writing for the Lord
MINISTRIES

Clarksville, Maryland (USA)

www.writingforthelord.com

Leadership with a Servant's Heart: *Leading in Your Workplace*
Retail Price: $24.95
©2022 by Kevin Wayne Johnson

Full Cover Concept by Kevin Wayne Johnson
Book Cover Design by Longtail Graphics c/o Carmelle Scott, Principal Designer
Baltimore, Maryland (USA)
(410) 361-0564

Edited by Daphne Parsekian
Norton Shores, Michigan (USA)
dparsekian@msn.com

Print and E-book distributed throughout the U.S.A., Canada, U.K./Europe, and Australia/New Zealand by INGRAM Book Company. Specific pricing added to include Brazil, China, Germany, India, Italy, South Korea, Poland, Spain, and Russia.

To order, call 1 (800) 937-8200.

All Rights Reserved. No part of this book may be reproduced by any mechanical, photographic, or electronic process or in the form of any audio recording. No part of this book may be stored in a retrieval system, transmitted, or otherwise copied for public or private use without prior written permission of the publisher – other than for "fair use" as brief quotations embodied in articles and reviews.

Unless otherwise noted, all Scripture references are taken from the King James, New King James, New International, New International Readers, the Message, Amplified, New Living Translation, the Living Bible, Easy-to-Read, or New Century Versions of the Holy Bible.

ISBN: 978-0-9883038-6-7
Library of Congress Catalog Number: 2022910425
Printed in the United States of America

Celebrating
Twenty-two Years of
Publishing Excellence

Writing for the Lord Ministries

Other Books by Kevin Wayne Johnson

Principal Author:

Give God the Glory SERIES

Topic: *FAITH*

Give God the Glory! series, winner of 19 literary awards (2001–2013) with selected books available in the following languages: Swahili, Urdu, Falam, Ngawn, Hungarian, and Georgian. Selected books in this series are available in the following formats as well: e-book and Amazon Kindle.

Know God and Do the Will of God Concerning Your Life ©2001

Called to Be Light in the Workplace ©2003

Let Your Light So Shine – A Devotional ©2004

The Godly Family Life ©2005

Your Role in Your Family – A Devotional ©2006

Know God and Do the Will of God Concerning Your Life – STUDY GUIDE ©2008

The Power in the Local Church ©2010

Know God and Do the Will of God Concerning Your Life – Revised Edition ©2011 [original publication 2001]

Called to Be Light in the Workplace – A WORKBOOK ©2013

Contributing Author:

Topic: *BOOK MARKETING*

> ***No Limits...No Boundaries:*** *Marketing Your Book Around the Globe*, with Antonio Crawford (*e-book*) ©2009

Topic: *FAITH*

> ***The Secret****: His Word Impacting Our Lives* ©2007

Topic: *FAMILY*

> ***Blended Families****: An Anthology* ©2006 [winner: Christian Small Publishers Association Book of the Year]
> ***The Soul of a Man 3:*** *I Can't Breathe*, with Elissa Gabrielle (*e-book*) ©2021

Topic: *FINANCE*

> ***Weekend Wealth Transfer:*** *How Black Churches Move Billions of Dollars out of Black Communities and How to Move It Back* ©2017

Topic: *WRITING*

> ***Christian Authors Unite:*** *Changing the Way Writers Write, Publish, and Think*, with Antonio Crawford ©2017
> ***Writing Is Essential****: Use the Skills You've Got to Get the Job Done* ©2019

Principal Author:

Topic: *SERVANT LEADERSHIP*

Leadership with a Servant's Heart series, winner of nine literary awards (2020–present). All books in this series are available in the following formats: e-book, Amazon Kindle, and audio.

> ***Leadership with a Servant's Heart***: *Leading through Personal Relationships* ©2019

Contributing Author:

Success Tips from Successful African Americans, *Volume 1*, with Everett Ofori ©2022

Next Level: Leaders XL, with Antonio Crawford ©2019

Praise for Leadership with a Servant's Heart

This book will equip you as a frontline worker, supervisor, department manager, or high-level executive. You can learn how to achieve your destiny by helping others to achieve theirs. Servant leadership coupled with life-long learning makes this book a literal training manual for effective personal, team, and organizational leadership.

— Dr. John Jackson
President, William Jessup University, Rocklin, California
www.jessup.edu
Author & Speaker on Leadership & Transformation
Trustees' Council, Lead Like Jesus

In *Leadership with a Servant's Heart: Leading in the Workplace*, Kevin Wayne Johnson provides a template for professionals who seek to authentically serve those they are called to lead. It provides a template that will allow you to develop your personal leadership skills while building the team around you. Whether you work in a corporate environment, church, not-for-profit, or government entity, your leadership is a part of your ministry. *Leading in the Workplace* is a great resource for your mentees and team members.

— LaKesha Womack
Founder, #RethinkingChurch Strategies LLC
Founding Member, Newsweek Expert Forum
Publisher, Ministry Matters Magazine
www.rethinkingchurchstrategies.com
Charlotte, NC

Leadership with a Servant's Heart: Leading in Your Workplace is a must-read. Once again, Kevin expounds on the importance of possessing a "Servant Leader Heart," especially while "surrendering" to the leading of the "Holy Spirit of God"! Kevin also shares (while role-modeling) the invaluable importance of learning from diverse generations in order to be a successful Servant Leader who teaches and serves others.

— **Gary McCants, Sr.**
Challenges of Faith Radio Program
100 Best Christian Podcasts (#49)
http://podsearch.com/listing/challenges-of-faith-radio-program.html
Crofton, Maryland

This book is designed to guide the hearts and actions of every Christ-like individual. It steers them into the path that Jesus Himself would take: servanthood – "If anyone should lead, let him first learn to be a servant." Author Kevin Wayne Johnson uses both testimonies and spiritual teachings to detail these points.

— **Lady Tracey**
The Lady Tracey Show
Radio Host (Unity Live Radio)
www.TopsRadioFM.com
www.UnityLiveRadio.co.uk
United Kingdom

Leadership with a Servant's Heart came to me at an opportune time. It will help you cultivate the spirit of daily reflection without which some great leaders have fallen. This book will help you rise to new heights, help you help others on their upward trajectory, and, together, while humble, stay perpetually at the top of your game!

— **Everett Ofori**
Book Editor
Prepare for Greatness: How to Make Your Success Inevitable
Success Tips from Successful African Americans, Volume I
Tsukuba, Ibaraki, Japan

Kevin Wayne Johnson has done and teaches that "leading in your workplace" is lovingly informing, instructing, and inspiring others to humbly perform at their peak. Every workplace leader would profit from practicing the principles shared in this book. I thank the triune God for Kevin Wayne Johnson's comprehensive contribution.

— **Reverend Sherwin E.S.A. Griffith**
Pastor, Castries Wesleyan Holiness Church, Castries, St. Lucia

Kevin Wayne Johnson shares practical and helpful insights on leadership in his latest book, ***Leadership with a Servant's Heart***, that will enrich, encourage, and challenge you in your leadership.

— **Gary Reinecke, MCC**
Co-Author of *Christian Coaching Essentials* and *Christian Coaching Excellence*
Co-Founder of <u>www.christiancoachingtools.com</u>
Executive Director, InFocus
Wildomar, California

Personal Reflections & Acknowledgments

I am very grateful to know that there is a true and living God. Throughout my lifetime, I have come to know and trust Him without wavering. Through this relationship, I accepted His only Son Jesus as my Lord and Savior on May 2, 1993, when my wife and I responded to the altar call during the Sunday morning church service at Full Gospel AME Zion Church, Temple Hills, Maryland. Upon receiving the infilling of the Holy Spirit, God's plan and purpose for my life became crystal clear. I am led and directed through my spiritual gifts of administration and leadership. If I did not have a relationship with God, I would not be an author or have much insight into the strategies and principles that govern good leadership.

This book series is a manifestation of many years of watching my dad lead as a United States Marine, enlisted and junior officer, and my late mom's urgent plea for me to seek a fulltime position with the federal government. I listened to Mom and served as a frontline, mid-level, and senior-level leader for thirty-four years prior to my retirement on October 31, 2017. In parallel, there are myriad ministry leaders whom I watched and listened to over a period of two decades who assisted in my growth and development so that I would serve well in multiple leadership positions in the local church. Thank you all for your commitment, dedication, tenacity, and sacrifice.

I am also extremely thankful for my wife, Gail, and three sons: Kevin, Chris, and Cameron. Leadership begins at home, and I learned so much of what I know through my family connection. An extension of my family includes my friendships with a plethora of fellow authors, publishing industry decision-makers, bookstore owners and managers, and book lovers everywhere that support my work.

— *Kevin*

Contents

*"But be very careful to keep the commandment and the law that Moses the servant of the L*ORD *gave you: to love the L*ORD *your God, to walk in obedience to him, to keep his commands, to hold fast to him and to serve him with all your **heart** and with all your soul."*

— Joshua 22:5 (NIV)

"Leaders are learners. Never allow your thirst to be quenched nor your hunger to be satisfied as it relates to lifelong learning. The more we grow through learning, the better equipped we are to pour into the lives of others. We were all created to serve, learn, and grow. When we do, we are walking in alignment with God's purpose. It is always more important to be prepared and not have an opportunity than it is to have an opportunity and not be prepared. The direct result of having the will to learn is a prepared servant...with a servant's heart."

— **Kevin Wayne Johnson**

The Scriptures define *heart* (*kardia*) in the context of Leviticus 17:11: "for the life of the flesh is in the blood." It occupies the most important place in the human body. Through an easy transition, the word came to stand for man's entire mental and moral activity, both the rational and the emotional elements. In other words, the *heart* is used figuratively for the hidden springs of the personal life.

The Bible describes human depravity as in the *heart* because sin is a principle that has its seat in the center of man's inward life and then "defiles" the whole circuit with its action (Matthew 15:19–20). On the other hand, the Scriptures regard the *heart* as the sphere of divine influence (Romans 2:15, Acts 15:9). The *heart*, as lying deep within, contains "the hidden man." In 1 Peter 3:4, this is the real man. It represents the true character but conceals it.

Sources: (a) *Vine's Complete Expository Dictionary of Old and New Testament Words*, W. E. Vine, Merrill F. Unger and William White, Jr., Thomas Nelson Publishers ©1996. (b) *Hastings Bible Dictionary*, J. Laidlaw

Introduction & Overview

Leadership with a Servant's Heart: *Leading Through Personal Relationships* was the beginning of a journey through a five-book series on the timely topic of servant leadership. Published and widely distributed in the fall of 2019, it earned praise from government officials, clergy, senior-level leaders in non-profit organizations, academia, and medium to large corporations. It earned nine literary awards in 2020 and 2021 from reputable and highly respected book reviewers as well as established publishing insiders and executives. I am grateful and honored that esteemed leaders and book lovers around the world valued its content.

Leadership with a Servant's Heart: *Leading in Your Workplace* continues the work that was begun and builds upon personal and professional relationships in the workplace. In 2021 more than 4.4 million Americans left their jobs due to varying levels of dissatisfaction as part of a movement that has become known as "The Great Resignation." The movement, which was highest among mid-career employees according to data compiled by the *Harvard Business Review*, sparked a flurry of activity among human resources managers and directors across multiple industries to address questions on how to retain talent. Erin Moran, Executive Director, Dr. Nancy Grasmick Leadership Institute at Towson University, Towson, Maryland, says, "The war for talent and finding great people is harder, more challenging, and more complicated than it ever has been before. It's the number one issue facing us. The people are the most precious resource. As companies compete to attract and retain talent, company culture is becoming an increasingly important selling point for employees. Money and compensation used to be the top tools used to attract and keep potential employees, but that is no longer the case." [1]

Key findings from the Association for Talent Development's 2019 "State of the Industry Report" published the following data that reveals verifiable data points about leadership development in our collective pursuits to attract and retain good talent in the workplace:

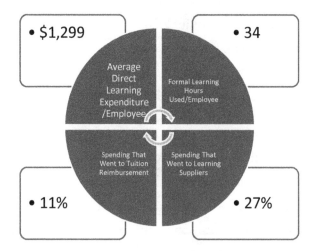

- $1,299 — Average Direct Learning Expenditure/Employee
- 34 — Formal Learning Hours Used/Employee
- 11% — Spending That Went to Tuition Reimbursement
- 27% — Spending That Went to Learning Suppliers

[2]

From this data, I have a few questions for your review and consideration as you begin to read this book:

» Are the dollars spent on leadership development generating a reasonable return on investment?
» Is the 11% tuition reimbursement too low to incentivize our employees?

» Are the internal training departments and staff adequately prepared to deliver leadership development training and programs, or should we continue to outsource this service at the current rate of 27%?

As for our faith and spirituality, a recent Gallup poll showed that fewer than half of Americans belong to a religious group. The percentage fell from 70% in 1999 to 47% in 2020—including some who once called themselves Christian. More and more of our citizens live their lives without regular interaction, encouragement, and instruction from God's Word through a local body of believers.[3]

This truth has a profound and life-changing impact on our *hearts*.

Whatever we do in word or deed begins in the *heart*. The heart is the foundation of our purpose, plans, motives, thoughts, values, and ambitions. True spiritual success in God's Kingdom requires a heart that is pure and clean, alive with eternal life, anointed of God, approved of God, and free from Code Red sin and disobedience. The heart has the power to determine our optimum levels of life and ultimately determines who we are in Christ and where we will spend eternity. It also controls our godly input and spiritual output. Heart failure manifests through disobedience, ignorance, and our own lack of understanding of our heart's condition, posture, and content. Even though God alone can change our heart, we are nevertheless responsible and accountable to Him for its condition. Our heart must be clean before it can be used by God. We must seek cleansing through faith. Afterward, the Lord keeps our heart secure in love and covered by grace and mercy.

As we enjoy God's excess of love, faith, and peace in our lives, there are five critical areas we need to give attention to if we are to avoid a wide gap between ourselves and God. All five of these are areas that deal with various aspects of the heart:

1. *Spiritual Heart Condition:* The basic condition we must fulfill is the requirement for a new heart, which only God can supply. While it is important to take care of our physical body, it is even more important to take care of our spirit. The regimen for a healthy spiritual heart is found in the Bible, God's spiritual health care guide.

2. *Heart Infiltration and Penetration:* The health of our spiritual heart depends on what we feed it. God seeks only our good and our optimum spiritual health. How close we are to God depends on how readily we allow His Word—His spiritual food—to enter our hearts and bear fruit in our lives.

3. *Spiritual Heart Consumption:* What we feed our heart is important because the heart is always hungry and will consume almost anything at any time. Unlike our natural heart, our spiritual heart is deceitful above all things (Jeremiah 17:9). This means that if we consume any ungodly thing, the heart will receive it and try to send us in the wrong direction.

4. *Spiritual Heart Response:* Thousands of different messages, both good and bad, bombard us every day. It is not always easy to know our own hearts or even our own response to those messages. A spiritual heart monitor is an indispensable

piece of equipment if we are to have any hope of closing the distance. That monitor is the Holy Spirit.

5. *Heart Meditation:* A great antidote against spiritual heart failure is deep meditation. To meditate means to ponder, study, muse, think over, and consider. Through deep meditation, we become more focused on God and can hear His voice more clearly. The key is to develop the habit of meditating from the heart on a daily basis, even during good times. The habit of meditation we develop during good times will carry over through the tough times.[4]

6. For three decades, I have been an avid reader of *Our Daily Bread*, published by Our Daily Bread Ministries (www.our-dailybread.org). In the April 2022 edition, author Bill Crowder reminds us that believers in Jesus live in two worlds with two citizenships. He also challenges us to think about this question: "How can we live out our heavenly citizenship here?" The answers provided are thought-provoking and life-changing, if applied. They are:

Pray for Leaders: "I urge, then, first of all, that petitions, prayers, intercession and thanksgiving be made for all people—for kings and all those in authority, that we may live peaceful and quiet lives in all godliness and holiness" (1 Timothy 2:1–2). This isn't an issue of philosophical agreement. It's a matter of spiritual responsibility. Our elected leaders deserve and need our prayers—whether we agree with their political positions or not.

Submit to Government Authority: "Let everyone be subject to the governing authorities, for there is no authority except that which God has established" (Romans 13:1). In the book of Daniel, we're reminded repeatedly (Daniel 4:17, 25, 32; 5:21) that God is sovereign over human activity but leaders are appointed by God according to His own purposes, whether or not we understand those purposes.

Render to Caesar: "Give back to Caesar what is Caesar's, and to God what is God's" (Matthew 22:21). Paul agrees with this is Romans 13:6–7, reminding us that human government has a role to play in God's economy and that we have a responsibility to support the workings of the governments and leaders of the nations in which we live.

Live an Honorable Life: "Show proper respect to everyone, love the family of believers, fear God, honor the emperor" (1 Peter 2:17). This isn't only being a good citizen; it also reflects the call of Christ to love our neighbors as ourselves (Matthew 22:39). By living honorably and showing honor to others—including those in government—we live as those who seek to honor God as well.

In addition to these direct responses to human government, believers in Christ also have the slightly more indirect challenge of living like Jesus wherever they reside. This involves the things that represent His *heart*—care for the poor, help for the weak, and justice for the oppressed.

All of this, however, exists with a significant qualifier. When threatened by leaders of the religious government of Israel, Peter wisely responded, "We must obey God rather than human beings!" (Acts 5:29). Our first allegiance is always to our Savior and His kingdom, for we are true citizens of Christ's kingdom, not merely resident aliens.

As you and your team read through the pages of **Leadership with a Servant's Heart:** *Leading in Your Workplace*, use your valuable time to self-reflect, self-assess, self-analyze, pause, meditate, and develop an action plan to address the systemic issues that require your attention. How will you influence change? I believe that you can make a positive impact wherever you work in the five major categories that comprise the workplace: government, corporate, academia, non-profits, or faith-based organizations. Together, let's be the leaders to show others how to lead with a servant's **heart.** It is my prayer that **Leadership with a Servant's Heart:** *Leading in Your Workplace* will take us there. Better leaders make the world a much better place.

Let's go!

---

[1] *I-95 Business* magazine, Stone House Media Group, Vicki Franz, Founder & Publisher, May 2022.
[2] The Association for Talent Development's 2019 State of the Industry Report.
[3] Billy Graham Evangelistic Association, April 22, 2021.
[4] *Code Red: Wars of the Heart*, by Bishop Dr. Donald R. Downing, Xulon Press, 2005, chapter 7, page 67, and chapter 12, pages 142–143.

PART ONE:

Servant Leadership – The Differentiator

If any man serve me, let him follow me; and where I am, there shall also my servant be: if any man serve me, him will my Father honour.

— John 12:26 (KJV)

1.
How Should We Serve Others?

PEOPLE WANT TO BE OUTSTANDING PERFORMERS
AND HIGH PRODUCERS. GIVE THEM A REASON
TO ACHIEVE THROUGH SERVICE.

*"You can get everything in life you want if you will
just help other people get what they want!"*

— Zig Ziglar (1926–2012)
World-Renowned Motivational Speaker

When I was a young man, my pastor taught me that "teaching is repeating until learning takes place." At the time, my church home, in Temple Hills, Maryland, was only fifteen minutes from my home, and I loved to attend every time that the doors were opened. The pastor's often repeated quote was a valuable lesson that continues to resonate with my interactions with my family, in the workplace, in my ministry assignments as I facilitate leadership development training and executive coaching as well as a positive lesson when I mentor others of all ages and experiences. It was one of the many ways that the pastor served the members during his tenure.

Serving others is a repetitive, ongoing, recurring, and continual process that requires our unwavering attention to detail until we witness transformation in the lives of others. It should be at the core of our being and an essential competency that comes easily and without constraint. In the Scriptures, Paul taught the Philippians, "Look not every man on his own things, but every man also on the things of others" (Philippians 2:4, KJV). However, we live in a dispensation of time that is not necessarily in alignment with this notion.

This chapter will offer some answers to the longstanding and proverbial question, "How should we serve others?" We will explore specific methods and review case studies that will encourage and motivate you to be a servant to those within your sphere of influence. The difference that you make in the lives of others is a step toward making your environment, and this world, a much better place.

Service Is the Ultimate Goal

Serving others brings fulfillment, joy, and a sense of satisfaction to all involved. The incredible benefits of service must be a documented goal as well as a desired outcome in the workplace. A servant is defined as one who serves others.[1] Though simplistic in its definition, in the context of servant leadership, its roots are derived from the Greek word *therapōn*, which means "to serve, to heal, an attendant, a servant and is a term of dignity and freedom." To add clarity to the goal of serving others, Paul shares an important message that, in essence, begins with the end in mind: Put the interests of others ahead of your own interests:

*Therefore if there is any **encouragement** and **comfort** in Christ [as there certainly is in abundance], if there is any consolation of **love**, if there is any **fellowship** [that we share] in the Spirit, if [there is] any [great depth of] **affection** and **compassion**, make my **joy** complete by being of the same mind, having the same [a]love [toward one another], knit together in spirit, intent on one **purpose** [and living a life that reflects your faith and spreads the gospel—the **good news** regarding salvation through faith in Christ]. Do nothing from selfishness or empty conceit [through factional motives, or strife], but with [an attitude of] **humility** [being neither arrogant nor self-righteous], regard others as more **important** than yourselves. Do not merely look out for your own personal interests, but also for the interests of others.*

– Philippians 2:1–4 (Amplified)

Paul emphasizes several words that positively influence those who read and hear them:

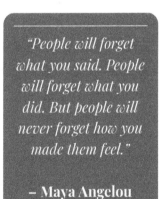

"People will forget what you said. People will forget what you did. But people will never forget how you made them feel."

– Maya Angelou

>> Encouragement – strength to move forward

>> Comfort – peace and tranquility

>> Love – an enduring concern for others

>> Fellowship – comradery, friendliness, and goodwill

>> Affection – an expression of caring for another

>> Compassion – empathy and valuing another's presence

» Joy – the emotion evoked by well-being, success
» or good fortune
» Good news – positive announcement of events
» Humility – to cease from unhealthy boasting or bragging
» Important – priority given

In the context of Paul's message, the book of Philippians is a thank you note to the believers at Philippi for their help in his hour of need, and he uses the occasion to send along some instruction on Christian unity. The message comes at a time when they need it most because fellow workers in the Philippian church are at odds and thus hindering their work and effectiveness. Paul encourages them through his writing and thanks them for their help, much like a servant leader should, as an expression of his love, appreciation, and thoughtfulness. Throughout this book, he freely expresses his fond affection for the Philippians, appreciates their consistent testimony and support, and lovingly urges them to center their actions and thoughts on the pursuit of the person and power of Christ. In doing so, he also seeks to correct the problems of disunity and rivalry (2:2–4) and to prevent the problems of legalism and antinomianism (3:1–19).

This epistle can serve as a reminder to current and future servant leaders. Like Paul, all leaders learn through observations, experiences, and life-transforming moments. Paul's past life (as Saul) was filled with wrath, disdain, and an unsettled spirit toward the church (Acts 8:3, 9:1–2). However, at a defined time and location, his attention was arrested, and his life was redirected toward a new assignment. All leaders have a personal testimony about someone who helped them to see the way and learn the characteristics and attributes of good leadership. For Paul, it was Jesus Himself (9:15–16). In some instances, the conversion is instantaneous, as with Paul (9:18–22). For others, it takes more time, and patience must prevail.

Coaching – An Approach Worth Adopting

A coach is a difference maker. The one-on-one relationship between a coach and the participant taps into the participant's potential and enables them to achieve much more than they could on their own. Once every four years, my family and I travel to the host city to witness the Summer Olympic Games. I attend about fifteen different sporting events during the two weeks of competition. In awe, I closely watch the world's most gifted athletes represent their respective nations in these events as they receive ongoing encouragement and inspiration from their coaches. I notice that the athletes that are encouraged by the most spirited coaches perform the best. Coaching, then, is an act of service because the coach puts the interest of their athlete ahead of their own agenda. The narrow margin of greatness between the top three athletes that compete for their nations and the athletes that finished in fourth place, not earning a position on the Olympic team, is the *coach*.

What skills should individuals have that will enable them to provide leadership in times of crisis? Resilience is one part of the equation. Clear communication, competence, calmness, and empathy are additional skills and traits of enormous importance. But how does one develop these capabilities? Professional coaching can make a remarkable difference and enable new thinking.

Kevin Wayne Johnson

Coaching is a thought-provoking partnership that supports employees and clients in reaching their fullest professional and personal potential. A coach is a thought partner, an accountability partner, and a catalyst that guides employees and clients toward clarity in their goals.

Coaches help employees and clients map the route to achieving these goals and producing favorable outcomes. A coach can work with an individual or team and help walk them through the natural states of fear and insecurity toward an openness to new possibilities. A professional coach is also trained to recognize whether additional support—trauma treatment, counseling, psychology— may also be necessary to lead through a crisis.

In times of crisis, or even peace, it is easy to focus only on what's happening right here, right now. With the assistance of a coach, organizational leaders can look further ahead and not only deal with the immediate emergency but also prepare for the coming changes. A coach can challenge assumptions and help leaders rechart their organization's future. That makes professional coaching an essential investment in effective crisis leadership for today and tomorrow.[2]

Coaching is defined as a helping relationship formed between a client that has managerial authority and responsibility in an organization and a consultant that uses a wide variety of behavioral techniques and methods to assist the client to achieve a mutually identified set of goals to improve his or her professional performance and personal satisfaction and, consequently, to improve the effectiveness of the client's organization within a formally defined coaching agreement.

A coach is a "thinking partner."

Prior to the start of all mentoring and coaching sessions, I suggest that the participants respond in writing to these five important questions. The preparation form that is presented to the participants should be the focus of the subsequent sessions toward the desired outcome:

1. What is the subject I want to discuss?
2. What do I want to achieve from this session?
3. What action have I taken since my last session with my last coach?
4. What do I want to be held accountable for?
5. What else would make this session the most productive and move me in the direction of my goals/objectives?

Diagram 1: Coaching vs. Mentoring – What's the Difference?

Diagram 1 is an aid to help understand the differentiations between coaching and mentoring. They are *Purpose, Role, Process, Relationship, Focus, Organizational Knowledge*, and *Skills Used*. A coach is a listener, thus offering a valuable service to the participant.

	Coach	Mentor
Purpose	Growth/development, helping while also generating results	Helping people realize their potential
Role	Learning/thinking partner	Learning/thinking partner, guide/expert

Process	Drawing out knowledge that resides within the participant Questioning: Coach engages in inquiry to guide the participant	Sharing knowledge that resides within a mentor Telling: Mentor shares expertise, offering answers and solutions
Relationship	Generally time-limited with a set duration	Ongoing relationship that can last for a long period of time
Focus	Helping participant develop their own way of problem solving	Helping mentee problem solve
Organizational Knowledge	May be somewhat limited, particularly if external coach	High level of knowledge about the organization
Skills Used	Listening, questioning, questioning, questioning	Listening, questioning, suggesting, advising, giving guidance

The Value Proposition of Coaching

» Participants are able to receive customized development activity under the guidance of a trained, certified coach.

» It helps to increase the pool of professionally trained coaches and will help your organization to push coaching further down into the organization.

» Once participants have exposure to some basic coaching skills, they start using them with their teams and explore their successes and challenges in their peer coaching triads, where they work with a coach to continue to develop their coaching skills.

» Following on from the initial session, participants are immediately aware that they are not buying some off-the-shelf personal development process. They're committing themselves to an ongoing and supportive relationship.

Diagram 2 (below) illustrates the unique nature of the coaching alliance and demonstrates where the power flows. Notice how the participant grants power to the relationship and is empowered by it and how the coach also grants power to the relationship; yet all the power returns to the participant, not the coach.

Diagram 2: The Coaching Relationship

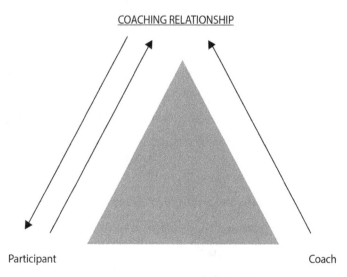

COACHING RELATIONSHIP

Participant   Coach

Adapted from source material by Whitworth, Kimsey-House, Sandahl

The diagram visualizes the actual working relationship—the unique nature of the coaching alliance—between the two parties. The participant is in control of how the coach serves them during this time of discovery so that potential is realized. This is because the coaching process has three underlying objectives:

- » Greater Awareness
- » Increased Responsibility
- » Greater Accountability

All three bring greater empowerment and resourcefulness to the participant, creating lasting change by adopting a learning approach that operates from the inside out as opposed to the outside in. Our potential cannot be found somewhere *outside* of us; it can only be discovered *within* us.[3]

Be a Role Model

In her insightful and thought-provoking article, "Leading with Character: Model the Way," Sandra L. Stosz shares a valuable lesson about servant leadership based upon the leadership style of a United States Coast Guard senior officer. She shares the following:

> "The closer I get to people, the more I love them. The further away I get from people, the more I judge them."
>
> – *John C. Maxwell*

Reflecting on the importance of emotional intelligence, executives must possess situational awareness to understand how their work habits and personal actions impact their people. Leading by example means creating a workplace climate that inspires subordinates to want to move up to take more responsible, demanding jobs. Supervisors who spend most of their time in the office and don't have a healthy work-life balance are probably not people who subordinates want to emulate. They may look up at their boss and think, "Wow, I don't want her job if that's what's expected."[4]

Stosz's article is a stark reminder of my humble beginnings and introduction to servant leadership. I began my thirty-four-year career with the federal government at the age of twenty-three, a few months after earning a Bachelor of Science degree from Virginia Commonwealth University School of Business. It was an exciting and life-changing time in my life. My first assignment and appointment was to a part-time position in the local Richmond, Virginia, district office of the Internal Revenue Service (IRS) as a taxpayer service representative. In this work role, I learned about customer service, the United States tax code, and how to professionally interact with the public. I remember the good training and efficient way the IRS treated us, but I do not remember much about the specific details and day-to-day operations during my six-month employment. Perhaps I was just too young to understand or appreciate the foundation that was before me.

Following this start of my federal government career, I successfully transitioned to full-time employment, exactly one week following my twenty-fourth birthday, after my acceptance into the Defense Logistics Agency's Centralized Intern Development Program, a three-year classroom and on-the-job training position for high potential entry-level employees. I was one of twenty-five new hires and future leaders across the country for this highly competitive opportunity. I reported for duty to the Defense Personnel Support Center in south Philadelphia on July 24, 1984, and the first person that I met was the program manager, Mr. Delma Hughes. He was a tall, kind, compassionate, pleasant, well-dressed, statuesque, and honorable man. He gained my immediate trust and confidence that I had made the right choice to accept entry into the program. Throughout my first year of the program, three-fourths of our time was in the classroom learning theory, regulations, strategies, principles, tips, nuggets, and tools that would govern our chosen career field: acquisition. The second person that I met was during my initial on-the-job training assignment in an office setting was Mrs. Catherine Ward, my supervisor. She was a serious yet gentle, attention-to-detail, experienced, seasoned, intelligent, and mother-like woman. How ironic because my mother gets the credit for encouraging me to apply for a federal government position—and I listened.

To this end, Mr. Hughes and Mrs. Ward were my first role models in the workplace. They were excellent teachers, mentors, and coaches at a time when I needed them the most. Unbeknownst to either of them, their influence and impact on my life was immeasurable, and I still try to model what they taught me as a twenty-four-year-old. What an impact! I speak highly of them both on numerous occasions.

Final Thoughts

In this chapter, we learned that people want to be outstanding performers and produce at a high level. As leaders, we have the responsibility to give them a reason to achieve through our *service*.

Chapter one asks a thought-provoking question: "How should we serve others?" Serving others has a mutually beneficial outcome for all involved, as illustrated by the Apostle Paul's transformation:

» As the one who serves others, you experience fulfillment, joy, and a sense of accomplishment. You were created to serve others.
» As the one being served, you feel appreciated, valued, cared for, and important.

A leader is a coach. Coaching provides opportunities to listen as others openly share and discuss what's on their hearts and minds. Good listening skills take time to develop, but once mastered, they are a means to demonstrate care and concern for others who may not have other venues to be heard. In doing so, we tap into their potential and help them to realize that oftentimes the answer they seek is already there. In essence, the coach encourages the participant to see their environment through a different lens.

Leaders live, work, and operate in a way that inspires others to achieve based upon character, integrity, and truth. A role model offers a visible manifestation of behaviors and mannerisms that are to be emulated. Set the tone, and be the example of what you expect to see in others. It is a powerful and life-transforming representation for others to see, live, and model. It begins with you. Mr. Hughes and Mrs. Ward showed me the way.

STUDY QUESTIONS and DISCUSSION

How Should We Serve Others?

1. Why is service to others so important, in your opinion?

    _____

    _____

    _____

    _____

    _____

2. What considerations do you afford to others that you are entrusted to lead?

    _____

    _____

    _____

    _____

    _____

3. Name two ways that you can serve others.

    _____

    _____

    _____

    _____

    _____

4. Do you believe that biblical principles guide your decisions? If so, list your top three.

_____

_____

_____

_____

_____

5. What can you do differently in your service to others?

_____

_____

_____

_____

_____

---

[1] The New Open Bible Study Edition, Thomas Nelson Publishers, 1990.

[2] "How Coaching Can Help You Move from Crisis Management to Crisis Leadership" by Magdalena Nowicka Mook, Chief Executive Officer, International Coaching Federation, May 5, 2021.

[3] Coaching Training, The John Maxwell Team, *The Art, Skill & Practice of Professional Coaching*, 2011, *The Mechanics of Coaching*, page 9.

[4] "Leading with Character: Model the Way," Sandra L. Stosz

2.
Understanding Generations

GENERATIONAL DIFFERENCES MUST BE
ACKNOWLEDGED AND ADDRESSED. LEADERSHIP
FINDS ITS SOURCE IN UNDERSTANDING.

*"Leaders must care. Leadership is about people. Period.
Great leadership is about inspiring people, serving people,
caring for people, and caring about people."*

— Gary Kelly
Former Chairman and CEO, Southwest Airlines

I am the eldest son of a United States Marine (retired). My dad is the eldest son of seven children, four boys and three girls. My dad, uncles, and aunts modeled several examples of good leadership for me as a child and throughout my adolescent and young adult years. They were born during the Traditionalist generation (pre-1945) and clearly exhibited most of that generation's core characteristics:

» Hardworking
» Willpower

- » Loyal employees
- » Respect authority
- » Waste not, want not
- » Tech-challenged
- » Traditional [1]

I was born during the Baby Boomer generation (1946–1964), married a baby boomer, and raised three sons who were born between 1995 and 1998. I passed on to my sons what I experienced and observed in terms of my generation's core characteristics:

> *"The greatest enemy of knowledge is not ignorance. It is the illusion of knowledge."*
>
> *– Stephen Hawking*

- » Strong work ethic
- » Self-assured
- » Competitive
- » Goal-centric
- » Resourceful
- » Mentally focused
- » Team oriented
- » Disciplined [2]

I noticed several similarities and differences in characteristics across the two generations. In this chapter, you will learn that these similarities and differences can be assets in the development of the team and organization alike.

The Leadership Challenge

Leaders have always known that uncertainty in the world, the workplace, and people's personal lives make shepherding an enterprise or team a daunting and complex challenge. Given the differences as it pertains to the generational gaps, the challenges of leading others are rooted in the following:

» Work experience
» Years of experience
» How we communicate, that is, preferred methods
» How we receive and process information
» Family upbringing
» What geographic regions of the country we have lived or currently live in
» Involvement in the local church or not
» Personality type
» Conflict management style
» Leadership style
» Emotional intelligence style
» Behavioral style
» Education level

Diagram 1. 4 Generations in the Workplace Today

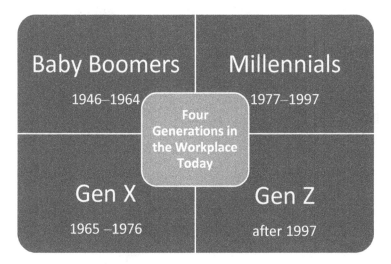

Compacted together in the workplace are four generations of people that represent different ethnicities, genders, cultures, and lifestyles. A leader will either embrace the diversity or allow the different approaches to solving problems and making decisions divide the team and organization. To this end, one generation of workers in particular is in line for mid-level and senior-level positions within their respective organizations: the millennials. This large group of men and women craves respect, value, and compassion from their leaders. The same must hold true as they lead as well. Employees at all levels in the workplace feel undervalued, marginalized, and underappreciated in more ways than one. U.S.-based companies spent $160 billion on employee training and education, yet:

» Fifty-eight percent of managers said they did not receive any *management training*.

» Seventy-nine percent of people quit their jobs due to *lack of appreciation*.

» Seventy-seven percent of organizations reported they are currently experiencing a *leadership gap*.

» Only ten percent of CEOs believe their company's leadership development initiatives have a *clear business impact*.

» Sixty-three percent of *millennials* said their leadership skills were not being *fully developed*.

What About the Millennials?

In his article titled "Millennials Overtake Baby Boomers as America's Largest Generation," author Richard Fry shares insightful data to help leaders at all levels in an organization better understand trends with regard to the largest generation and how it impacts the workplace.

Millennials have surpassed baby boomers as the USA's largest living adult generation, according to population estimates from the United States Census Bureau. As of July 1, 2019, millennials, whom we define as ages 23 to 42 in 2019, numbered 72.1 million, and boomers (ages 55 to 73) numbered 71.6 million. Generation X (ages 43 to 54) numbered 65.2 million and is projected to pass the boomers in population by 2028.

The millennial generation continues to grow as young immigrants expand its ranks. Boomers—whose generation was defined by the boom in U.S. births following World War II—are aging and their numbers shrinking in size as the number of deaths among them exceeds the number of older immigrants arriving in the country.

Diagram 2. Projected Population by Generation

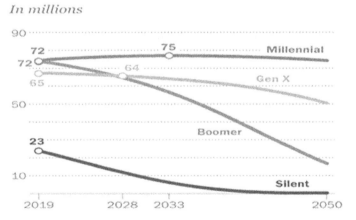

Projected population by generation

In millions

Note: Millennials refer to the population ages 23 to 38 as of 2019.
Source: Pew Research Center tabulations of U.S. Census Bureau population estimates released April 2020 and population projections released December 2017.

PEW RESEARCH CENTER

Because generations are analytical constructs, it takes time for popular and expert consensus to develop as to the precise boundaries that demarcate one generation from another. In early 2018 Pew Research Center assessed demographic, labor market, attitudinal, and behavioral measures to establish an endpoint—albeit inexact—for the millennial generation. Under this updated definition, the youngest millennial was born in 1996.

Here's a look at some generational projections:

Millennials

» With immigration adding more numbers to this group than any other, the millennial population is projected to peak in 2033 at 74.9 million. Thereafter, the oldest millennial will be at least 52 years of age, and mortality is projected to outweigh net immigration. By 2050 there will be a projected 72.2 million millennials.

Diagram 3. The Generations Defined

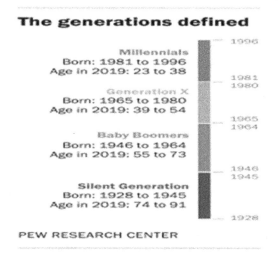

The generations defined

Millennials
Born: 1981 to 1996
Age in 2019: 23 to 38

Generation X
Born: 1965 to 1980
Age in 2019: 39 to 54

Baby Boomers
Born: 1946 to 1964
Age in 2019: 55 to 73

Silent Generation
Born: 1928 to 1945
Age in 2019: 74 to 91

PEW RESEARCH CENTER

Diagram 4. Births Underlying Each Generation

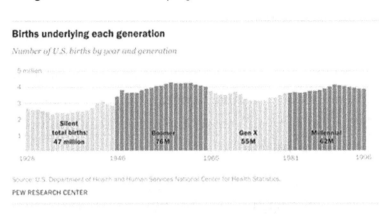

Births underlying each generation
Number of U.S. births by year and generation

Source: U.S. Department of Health and Human Services National Center for Health Statistics.
PEW RESEARCH CENTER

Generation X

» For a few more years, Gen Xers are projected to remain the "middle child" of generations—caught between two larger generations, the millennials and the boomers. Gen Xers were born during a period when Americans were having fewer children than in later decades. When Gen Xers were born, births averaged around 3.4 million per year, compared with the 3.9 million annual rate from 1981 to 1996 when the millennials were born.

» Gen Xers are projected to outnumber boomers in 2028, when there will be 63.9 million Gen Xers and 62.9 million boomers. The Census Bureau estimates that the Gen X population peaked at 65.6 million in 2015.

Baby Boomers

» Baby boomers have always had an outsize presence compared with other generations. They peaked at 7.8 million in 1999 and remained the largest living adult generation until 2019.

» By midcentury, the boomer population is projected to dwindle to 16.2 million.[3]

For millennials (currently the largest generation), "leadership means trust, empathy, and empowerment," says Gertrud Kohl, staff member at Brunswick in Frankfurt, Germany. Further, she shares that "communication styles of younger workers point the way to a more effective managerial style."

Long years of service and experience count for little if you can't communicate effectively with your team—and that means understanding how they communicate with each other. As a leader, you must be prepared to make the most of the rapid-fire changes in corporate communications. Some of them may not be obvious.

The older generation, who have naturally assumed leadership positions based on long years of experience, are the ones most at risk of falling behind—ignoring the implications of a particular medium or mode of communicating that millennials and younger employees understand intuitively. They represent the fastest-growing and probably the largest part of your workforce.

As digital natives, they recognize the differences in styles of communication intuitively. A leader offering a simple "Great job!" to an employee on LinkedIn or liking an employee's post means something different than an internal congratulatory email. A seemingly off-the-cuff tweet on Twitter may carry more weight with some audiences than a carefully worded press release.

But such differences also represent a different way of being in the world, a different set of expectations for communication and leadership. Being able to navigate these spheres effectively is not a superficial skill but an expression of caring—a message in itself.

For leaders, that is an important insight. The thought and time it takes to create an engaging post on a particularly relevant medium go a long way toward demonstrating that a leader understands the world their employees live in. And it also points out how other aspects of the boss–employee relationship might benefit from a refreshed approach to communication.

Millennials are seeking specific attributes to be at their best. They are as follows:

Communication – Writing in 1989, U.S. researchers Kevin Barge and Randy Hirokawa determined that communication must actually be considered a prerequisite of leadership. "Leadership occurs through the process of interaction and communication," they wrote. Similarly, German researcher Anja Blaschke, in 2008, discovered that "leading people means communicating with them"—a seemingly obvious point, all too easily overlooked in the moment. In 2002 researchers David Clutterbuck and Sheila Hirst defined leadership by the quality of communication: "Leaders who do not communicate well are not really leading at all. It is one thing to have the position, another to fulfill the role."

Many employees regard their own supervisor as the most important communication partner in the company, church, or organization. And today, those supervisors act as advisors in all matters, as motivators and role models, and as sparring partners for common issues. This represents an important time commitment—making direct, dynamic involvement with employees a priority in the workweek. Moderating team meetings and distributing tasks are by no means enough.

Successful leadership communication can be defined as a very personal phenomenon that helps define the relationship between superiors and employees; it expresses itself situationally and is a two-way street—neither completely leader nor follower centered. Rather, a constructive leadership style must emphasize shared values and objectives. The year 2020 was a critical test in that respect. The increasing pace of change in the work environment over the last decade has increased the demands on leadership communications, and the coronavirus pandemic has only shifted that process into a higher gear. With most employees working remotely, there is greater pressure for leadership styles to be creative. With communication being a fundamental component of leadership, one could assume leaders within the communications industry would certainly understand the terms. Yet even there, young workers seem dissatisfied with their bosses in many cases, as a study conducted by the University of Leipzig under the direction of Prof. Dr. Ansgar Zerfass showed in 2020. His research, as Chair of Strategic Communications, found that just under half of the respondents (46.6%) said that their immediate supervisor would be a good leader, while 33.6% were partially satisfied and 19.8% complained about poor leadership quality.

Born in the 1980s or later, these workers have grown up in the milieu of social media. They are used to participating in every discussion and having their concerns acknowledged and appreciated. They are fluent enough in the languages of social media that they will reflexively judge the tone of a communication and spot insincerity in an instant. Naturally, these employees are going to have fairly specific expectations of leadership. A leadership style appropriate for baby boomers and Gen-Xers doesn't work well for them and could prove counterproductive to your business. On the other hand, what works for them can also enrich leadership communications with the older generation.

Trust – All people have a primal desire for trust. This applies to relationships of all kinds, including leadership relationships. And it isn't generation specific. We all strive for trust that is gained through respect and appreciation for us and our work.

To build a trusting relationship, leaders should communicate openly, authentically, and honestly at all times and expect the same in return. This does not mean that leaders must know many private details of their employees' lives to communicate openly with them, but it does mean that in the work context, relevant activities, projects, processes, challenges, and problems—and, yes, also mistakes—must be discussed as transparently as possible. Mistakes happen. We are all human. What is crucial is the way we deal with them.

Listening and flexibility are crucial to building trust. Young workers want their supervisors to provide them with a structure where they can feel safe and where they can safely share their thoughts and be heard. They don't want to be monitored at every step but rather to be trusted to do their best. Flexibility and transparency generate trust in leadership communication and can ultimately lead to a better work performance.

<u>Empathy</u> – Leaders are more and more often seen as important coaches. That doesn't mean they have an answer to every question. Instead, they help guide their employees to the right question and a path to finding the answer. In his *Harvard Business Review* article, John Hagel III notes this approach requires a certain realistic humility: "You think you have the answers to all important questions? That suggests that you are either clueless—you have no idea how rapidly the world is changing—or that you are lying. In either case, you won't find that trust that you've been looking for."[4] This aspect of trust building is all about empathy, the art of being able to put yourself in other people's shoes. To build up an honest, emotional relationship with employees, the leader's ability to empathize is indispensable—especially when dealing with younger generations, which are even more eager to experience genuine support for their own professional and private development.

Empathetic leadership must include negative criticism, of course, or it risks appearing dishonest. People want to receive not only positive but also appropriate negative feedback. In a typical team, not everyone's wishes and expectations can be achieved. The leader decides how to achieve a common good and guides the team members toward it in the most constructive way possible.

<u>Empowerment</u> – The Deloitte Millennial Survey 2019 found that just under half of the millennials surveyed would leave their job within the next two years if given the opportunity. For about a third, the reason would be a lack of opportunities to learn, grow, and develop.

From a leader perspective, providing the kind of atmosphere where growth can occur can be a bit scary. It means letting go of the reins, handing over responsibility, and empowering your employees. But true empowerment means not just granting them the freedom to act but also encouraging them and motivating them toward successful achievement. This gives them the opportunity to grow, a greater appreciation for the work, and a greater sense of personal accomplishment. Upon completion, detailed feedback sessions where leaders and employees can exchange views about the project can build confidence in the approach for both sides. After all, leaders need critical feedback too; they want to develop and enhance their leadership skills.

Leadership across the board benefits from these foundational practices, regardless of the age of your employees. One of the goals of leadership should be to foster a healthy interaction among the various generations represented by your team. Reverse mentoring can be a constructive option if, for example, the boss is a non-digital native that needs to catch up in terms of digital communication.[5]

To honor and engage with your employees in this way, through trust, empathy, and empowerment, is to see them for who they are and who they can be, to maximize their potential as individuals and as a team. Success means you've also maximized your effectiveness as a leader.[6]

The Pandemic (Coronavirus) Propelled the Talent Shortage to New Heights

Research conducted and distributed by Portico Consulting LLC reveals the following impacts and how changed behaviors among these generational groups as a whole were influenced by the coronavirus pandemic:

Diagram 5. Generations Most Affected and Impacts

Generation(s) Most Affected	Impact
Millennials and Generation Z	It changed the way work gets done, if they want to work, how they want to work, when they want to work, and what kind of work they want.
Millennials and Generation Z	The "Mission Factor" is important to the younger workforce. They value purpose over paycheck. Work must fit into their lives!
Millennials and Generation Z	Before the pandemic, they were already losing the connection between "Work and Pay."
Millennials and Generation Z	The pandemic aid allowed/afforded a lifestyle that aligned with their values and work style.
All	Millions in the U.S. collected $4,000–$5,000 per month for not working, plus there were many financial aid programs.
Millennials and Generation Z	With remote work, we moved further away from transformational communication and closer to transactional communication.

All	We are now competing for talent, with many who want to work when they want to work and how they want to work, and they like remote work settings.

7

Understanding these differences and the associated impacts will help leaders at all levels better understand how to attract and retain top talent across multiple work roles for the foreseeable future.

Help Others Understand the "Why"

The book of Proverbs is the most intensely practical book in the Old Testament because it teaches skillful living in the multiple aspects of everyday life. The key word in this book is *wisdom*. It is defined as the ability to live life skillfully. A godly life in an ungodly world, however, is no simple assignment. Proverbs provides God's detailed instructions for His people to deal successfully with the practical affairs of everyday life, that is, how to relate to:

» God.
» Parents.
» Children.
» Neighbors.
» Government.
» One another.

Proverbs is one of the few biblical books that clearly spells out its purpose. The purpose statement in Proverbs 1:2–6 is twofold:

1. To impart moral discernment and discretion (1:3–5) and
2. To develop mental clarity and perception (1:2, 6).

The words "wisdom" and "instruction" in 1:2 complement each other because *wisdom (hokhmah)* means "skill," and *instruction (musar)* means "discipline." No skill is perfected without discipline, and when a person has skill, he has freedom to create something beautiful. It is a book that touches upon every facet of human relationships, and its principles transcend the bounds of time and culture. Wisdom is more than shrewdness or intelligence. Instead, it relates to practical righteousness and moral acumen.[8]

To this end, a leader can positively influence the outcome of any conversation, policy statement, directive, or request by helping others to understand the "why." The why is key to helping those within our sphere of influence understand how we arrived at a decision and how we chose to solve a particular issue, concern, or problem. Scripture helps us to embrace this realism: "Wisdom is the principal thing; therefore get wisdom: and with all thy getting get understanding" (Proverbs 4:7, KJV). Wisdom is greater than knowledge, acumen, or intelligence. Wisdom is the wise application of what we know and understand as subject matter experts in our chosen fields. As we utilize the wisdom that has been granted to us as leaders, it aids in our understanding. This in turn allows us to focus on the how and why a decision was derived in lieu of the decision itself. This way, all personal and professional relationships can be maintained even if disagreement persists. During the process of ensuring that others understand the why, two-way communication has most likely occurred, good listening skills have been on display, mutual respect has been achieved, and honor for another's point of view and perspectives has been realized. When leaders also take the time to demonstrate a genuine concern for another's viewpoints and carefully listen to them, we gain their buy-in even when they do not agree.

Diagram 6. Giving Your Perspective – What to Say and How to Say it

Albert Mehrabian's research points to the importance of how you deliver your message, considering tone of voice and body language, and tailoring your message to the needs of the receiver. It involves:

» Delivering the content of your message with clarity and completeness.
» Using the appropriate tone of voice and body language.
» Framing the message to account for the needs and interests of the receiver.

When determining what to say, remember the two criteria for delivering the content of the message: (1) be complete, and (2) be clear.

The elements of a complete message are above in Diagram 6, and the elements of delivering a clear message are:

» Getting to the point and not beating around the bush.
» Avoiding jargon, acronyms, or slang that others may not understand.
» Organizing the message with a logical structure.

However, the why ushers in understanding. The why is the rationale behind the message.

When leaders make the effort to seek understanding of their decisions, they earn greater trust and influence.

Final Thoughts

Chapter two begins with a leadership challenge. Understanding generations is an acknowledgement and recognition that there is a rich and diverse dynamic in the workplace that leaders must tap into to get the best results for the team and the organization at large.

In this chapter, we learned that generational

differences must be understood first and addressed second. Leadership finds its source in understanding. As we delve into these differences, we put ourselves in a position as leaders to embrace and celebrate these differences that shape the personalities and styles of people within our spheres of influence:

» Years of work experience

» Levels of educational experience
  - High school only
  - Undergraduate degree
  - Graduate degree
  - Doctorate degree
» Family upbringing
» Geographic region of the country (where we grew up)
» Personality type

All of the above are key determinants of how people react to situations and how they communicate with others.

Millennials currently represent the largest generation in the U.S. (72.1 million). Leaders must give considerable thought and develop plans of action to address their most pressing concerns as they serve or move into those critically important mid-level and, in some instances, senior-level positions of responsibility. We learned:

» They will remain the largest generation through 2050.
» Leadership means trust, empathy, and empowerment.
» Long years of service and experience count for little if you can't communicate effectively.
» They also value empathy and empowerment.

Lastly, we learned that Proverbs 4:7 teaches leaders, "...with all thy getting get understanding." Maintaining healthy and productive personal and professional relationships is rooted in helping others to understand why we make decisions and solve problems.

STUDY QUESTIONS and DISCUSSION

Understanding Generations

1. Why do you think that generational differences can lead to unity?

    _____

    _____

    _____

    _____

    _____

2. What steps have you taken to acknowledge differences among generations in the workplace?

    _____

    _____

    _____

    _____

    _____

3. How would you get a Generation Xer and a millennial to work together cohesively?

    _____

    _____

    _____

    _____

    _____

4. How important are differences in work experience in leading others? Give an example.

_____

_____

_____

_____

_____

5. How do you measure your effectiveness in bridging gaps among generations?

_____

_____

_____

_____

_____

[1] www.thebalancecareers.com

[2] www.elearningindustry.com

[3] "Millennials Overtake Baby Boomers as America's Largest Generation," by Richard Fry (Pew Research), April 28, 2020.

[4] "Good Leadership Is About Asking Good Questions," *Harvard Business Review*, by John Hagel III, January 8, 2021.

[5] The Deloitte Millennial Survey 2019, "Societal Discord and Technological Transformation Create a Generation Disrupted," www.deloitte.com

[6] "For Millennials, Leadership Means Trust, Empathy, Empowerment," by Gertrud Kohl, Brunswick, Frankfurt, Germany, June 2, 2021.

[7] *"The Pandemic (Coronavirus) Propelled the Talent Shortage to New Heights,"* Research conducted and distributed by Portico Consulting LLC.

[8] The New Open Bible Study Edition, Thomas Nelson Publishers, 1990, pages 701–702.

3.

Perception Versus Reality: How Leaders Inspire

ADDING VALUE TO PEOPLE HELPS THEM
TO REACH THEIR FULL POTENTIAL.

*"A successful person finds the right place for himself.
But a successful leader finds the right place for others."*

— John C. Maxwell
The world's #1 leadership expert

During the summer of 2017, I accepted an invitation from the president of the Interstate Fellowship of Churches to lead the men's fellowship portion at their annual summer camp with a group of church leaders and their respective members from the states of California, Washington, Oregon, Arizona, and Nevada. The three-day summer camp, held in July, was in Hansford, California, about ten miles from Fresno. I was truly inspired and honored to receive this invitation and prayed that I would be an inspiration to the men in attendance.

Prior to departing Baltimore-Washington International (BWI) Airport on a Thursday evening, I received a text message from Delta Air Lines informing me that there would be a delay with my connecting flight in Salt Lake City, Utah. A few hours later, when I landed in Salt Lake City (SLC), I comfortably proceeded to the food court for a scrumptious meal with the understanding that the connecting flight to Fresno would be delayed. I did not bother to confirm or validate the text message that I had received at BWI. After I finished my meal, I proceeded to my assigned gate only to discover that the connecting flight to Fresno did indeed depart on time. I was not notified but should have checked anyway.

My limited options at this time of the evening to arrive at my destination on schedule were to rent a car at the SLC airport, reserve a seat on a bus line, or wait until the next morning to board an early flight. Of these three options, the only viable one was to rent a car and drive eleven hours over night because my session was scheduled to start at 10:00 a.m. Through prayer, I asked God to help me to arrive safely and on time for my assignment. As always, He answered my prayer so that I would arrive energetic and ready to deliver the message that I had prepared for the men. Someone needed to be inspired.

In this chapter, you will learn that inspiration—the art of inspiring others—will propel your team and organization to new heights. Let's explore how and why it is so effective in the lives of those that you are entrusted to lead.

A Dire Need for Action

Employees at all levels in the workplace feel undervalued, marginalized, and underappreciated in more ways than one. One's perception is also one's reality.

From the perspective of leaders, companies around the world are facing a leadership crisis, according to the new quarterly report of the 2021 Global Leadership Forecast that was released on May 12, 2021. Only 11% of surveyed organizations reported they have a "strong" or "very strong" leadership bench, the lowest it has been in the past ten years.

The crisis can be traced to a failure by companies to provide leadership development and transition training for newly hired and current executives, according to Development Dimensions International (DDI), which conducts the annual survey. The highest global average rating for bench strength was 18% in 2011. It has been on the decline ever since. The DDI survey was conducted between February 2020 and July 2020. It includes data from more than 15,000 leaders and 2,100 human resource professionals who represent 1,740 organizations in twenty-four industries globally. Other major findings from the survey:

» Twenty-eight percent of organizations with high-quality development had a strong leadership bench. Combining assessment with development delivered even higher bench strength. On average, combining high-quality assessment with any development program boosts bench strength by 30%.

» Nearly 40% of organizations with both high-quality development and assessment had a strong bench of leaders ready for critical roles.

» Stress wrecks leaders' confidence levels. Nearly half of leaders with stressful transitions rated themselves as average to below-average leaders. One in sixteen C-level executives said their transitions were so stressful they often thought about quitting.

Fewer than 20% of organizations have a bench of capable leaders ready to fill critical roles. The results signal that leadership development is the most important step companies can take to drive executive success and long-term bench strength.[1]

Acknowledge Reality (The Talent Shortage)

I serve on the Board of Directors for the non-profit national organization Nexus Family Healing, Plymouth, Minnesota, whose mission is "Restoring Hope. Reshaping Futures." Their phenomenal work is three-fold as they advocate for and support at-risk youth as well as their immediate and extended families:

» Outpatient/community mental health services
» Residential treatment programs
» Foster care and adoption services

I received the invitation to serve on the Board of Directors from the Chief Executive Officer, Dr. Michelle Murray, following my keynote speech at their 2017 annual training conference. While I was honored and eventually accepted the invitation, I did so to learn, understand, work with, and help the leadership team to realize the mission, vision, and strategic direction for the future. I am the brother of a mentally disabled sibling and father of an autistic son. I can relate to why Nexus exists, and I knew that I would learn so much about inspiring others from the services that they provide across the U.S. through their multiple local facilities. At one of our Board of Director meetings, a consultant led a conversation titled "The Talent Shortage."[2] While much of the dialogue focused on the health care and trauma-informed profession, we left with a broader understanding of a current dilemma and the need to inspire workers to make a change.

Where Are We Right Now?

» The huge cache of available jobs is not being filled very rapidly. Businesses are losing revenues because they don't have enough staff to produce goods and services.[3]

» A record number of people are quitting their jobs. Nearly four million people quit their jobs in April 2021.[4]

» Workers are pickier about jobs they accept. Getting people to return to work, take a job, and/or stay working once they are hired is tied to several challenges:

- A change in worker mentality.
- A wave of early retirements.
- A lack of child-care options
- A lingering fear of the coronavirus
- Generous unemployment benefits and many government subsidy programs [5]

» The talent shortage is global. By 2030 the global talent shortage is predicted to reach 85.2 million. Businesses worldwide risk losing $8.4 trillion in revenue because of the lack of skilled talent.[6]

The Basis of the Talent Shortage Was Here Before the Pandemic

» Birth rate
  - The birth rate has decreased.
  - In 1980 the birth rate was 15.9 per 1,000. In 2020 the rate is 11.41 per 1,000[7]
» Death rate
  - In 2020, 869.7 per 100,000
  - The death rate has increased.
  - In 1980 the death rate was 878.3 per 100,000. From 1980 to approximately 2010, the death rate was declining.
  - However, from about 2011 to 2020, it has been increasing. The rate of deaths per 100,000 is approximately the death rate in 1980.[8]
» Students studying STEM fields
  - The rate of college enrollments in science, technology, engineering, and mathematics is declining and will have a significant negative impact on our ability to access technical talent.[9]
  - Students in STEM programs are likelier than those in non-STEM fields to change majors. Example: 52% of students who initially declared as math majors ended up majoring in something else.[10]

These data and statistics serve as motivators to inspire others in the workplace, particularly the current and next generation of leaders.

How Will You Be Remembered?

Prison is the last place from which to expect a letter of encouragement, but that is where Paul's second letter to young Timothy originates. He begins by assuring Timothy of his continuing love and prayers and reminds him of his spiritual heritage and responsibilities. Timothy has Paul's example to guide him and God's Word to fortify him as he faces growing opposition and glowing opportunities in the last days. In essence, Paul urges Timothy on to steadfastness in the fulfillment of his divinely appointed task. After all, only the one who perseveres, whether as a soldier, athlete, farmer, or minister of Jesus Christ, will reap the reward.

In chapter three of the book of 2 Timothy, Paul encourages young Timothy, through his writing, to remain loyal and committed to his assignment. He emphasizes to Timothy not to fall away from God. Paul's words remind him about the coming of apostasy and how to confront it. Paul writes:

> All Scripture is God-breathed [given by divine inspiration] and is profitable for instruction, for conviction [of sin], for correction [of error and restoration to obedience], for training in righteousness [learning to live in conformity to God's will, both publicly and privately—behaving honorably with personal integrity and moral courage]; so that the [a]man of God may be complete and proficient, outfitted and thoroughly equipped for every good work. – 2 Timothy 3:16–17 (Amplified)

This writing is motivating, inspiring, and encouraging in its intent, context, and messaging. A key takeaway is that the messaging can, and should, be applied to our personal and professional development—in the family, in the home, in the church, in the workplace, and in the social and civic organizations where we all congregate. There are seven key messages that are extracted from this passage of Scripture:

1) **All** Scripture is God-breathed. God is intimately involved and orchestrated every word that is recorded in the Holy Bible. Combined with a proper attitude, His Word will direct, encourage, satisfy, and guide us. In the book of Psalms, the psalmist wrote these comforting passages of Scripture in chapter 119:

    a. Psalm 119:105 – God's Word lights our path.

    b. Psalm 119:106–108 – Instruction on how to please God

    c. Psalm 119:109 – God's Word encourages us in affliction.

    d. Psalm 119:110 – God's Word helps us not to stray from His truth.

    e. Psalm 119:111 – God's Word gives us joy.

2) It is given by divine **inspiration.**

    a. Psalm 119:160 – It builds trustworthiness because God's Word is true from the beginning.

    b. Isaiah 55:11 – God's Word will accomplish what He pleases, and it shall prosper in the thing where He sends it.

    c. Psalm 139:17 – David reminds us that God's thoughts of us are precious.

3) It is profitable for **instruction**, the act of imparting knowledge to others.

    a.   Jeremiah 32:33 – It is given by God.

    b.   Proverbs 1 – God compels us to obey our parents, avoid bad company and seek wisdom. In verse 3, He specifically teaches us "to receive the instruction of wisdom, justice, and judgment, and equity."

4) **Conviction** makes one conscious of their guilt.

    a.   John 16:7–11 – It is produced by the Holy Spirit.

    b.   Psalm 51:1–17 – It is revealed by David through his confession of sin and request for forgiveness.

5) **Correction** is symbolic of punishment designed to restore.

    a.   Proverbs 29:17 – God's comforting words ensure, "He shall give you rest and he shall give delight unto thy soul."

    b.   Proverbs 3:12 – The Lord loves whom He corrects.

    c.   Job 5:17 – Eliphaz encourages Job not to despise God's discipline. His Word says, "Behold, happy is the man whom God corrects."

6) **Training** in righteousness is for the purpose of keeping us in right standing with God and uprightness before God. Three kinds of righteousness are revealed in Philippians:

    a.   2:6 – Legal. Christ's example of humility is illustrated in knowing that He was equal with God.

    b.   2:9 – Personal and imputed. Through Christ's act of humility and obedience, God exalted Him and gave Him a name that is above every name

7) We are thoroughly **equipped** for every good work. Ephesians 2:10 (Amplified) says , "For we are His workmanship [His own master work, a work of art], created in Christ Jesus [reborn from above—spiritually transformed, renewed,

ready to be used] for **good works**, which God prepared [for us] beforehand [taking paths which He set], so that we would walk in them [living the **good** life which He pre-arranged and made ready for us]."

As a leader, you will discover that your followers

appreciate your attention to detail and the time that you take to pour into their lives and provide opportunities for their growth and development. They will remember you for these small yet important deeds. Equally important, they will be inspired.

Dr. David Griffin, a former fire captain, recently shared an insightful lesson about how the Charleston, South Carolina, battalion chief and shift commander led his direct reports. He tells his story as follows:

> I heard the Rascal Flatts singing a song titled, "How They Remember You," with over one million views on YouTube.com, the other day that really affected my thoughts as a leader. I realized that whether we like it or not, as leaders, we'll be remembered. My question to you is, how will you be remembered? Here's an excerpt from the song. What does it say to you?
>
> > *You're gonna leave a legacy no matter what you do*
> > *It ain't a question of if they will*
> > *It's how they remember you*
> > *Did you stand or did you fall?*
> > *Build a bridge or build a wall?*
> > *Hide your love or give it all?*
> > *What did you do? What did you do?*

Did you make them laugh or make them cry?
Did you quit or did you try?
Live your dreams or let them die?
What did you choose? What did you choose?
When it all comes down
It ain't if, it's how they remember you

Interestingly enough, plenty of leaders say that they don't want to be or care whether they're remembered. However, you will be remembered for the good and the bad.

"You're gonna leave a legacy no matter what you do."

Your legacy evolves every shift that you go to work, every interaction that you have with your teammates on or off duty. How do you speak with your team? How do you help your team solve problems? Do you support them and show interest in their work and their personal lives? Do you take time to check on them to see how they're doing? Do you take time to share a meal or a cup of coffee with them? Are you brave enough to let them vent? Do you know your department's policies as you should to support them? Are you engaged in the work of your department to help to improve it for them? Is your skill set where it needs to be in your position?

All of these questions dictate how you will be remembered and whether you made a difference in your teammates' lives. After all, as a leader, isn't that your most important role?

"Did you stand or did you fall?" This is an important one. Do you have a code? What do you stand for? Your teammates

know whether you stand for something. Your teammates know whether you'll help them in difficult situations either on an emergency scene or in an administrative setting. If you don't have a code as a leader and stand for what's right, rather than who's right, then how do you expect your teammates to do this? You set this example daily, and you must be cognizant of that, because they are watching, as they should be.

"Build a bridge or build a wall?" Do you build bridges between the different companies, shifts, ranks, etc., in your department? Do you work with automatic aid and mutual aid through the good and the bad? Are you willing to take the advice of someone in the firehouse who might have a good idea even if that individual has less time on the job than you have?

These are very simple actions that can build relationships, but you must be willing, as a leader, to make the effort. If you don't, how do you expect the people you are responsible for to do so?

"Hide your love or give it all? What did you do?" This one might be difficult for you. You are hardened by this job, and in some cases, this doesn't allow you to show your love for the people whom you serve with. Now, I know that it's a different kind of love, but it still is an emotion that you have for your teammates. (Well, at least I hope that you have that.) How do you show this? Do you say thank you to your teammates? Do you tell them that you appreciate them? Do you give them positive reinforcement along with positive documentation that goes in their personnel file? This takes time and effort, but it's essential.

How can you serve your teammates in a profession where you have your life in each other's hands and not have a deep sense of caring for them? Your teammates can tell whether you care for them.

"Did you make them laugh or make them cry?" There are times to be serious and times to keep it light. As a leader, you must be able to balance these two. If you always are serious, your teammates won't be able to relax around you. If they can't relax around you, it will be difficult to get to know them and to really understand what makes them tick. If you can't understand what makes them tick, then you will have a difficult time leading them inside and outside of the firehouse.

Throw out a joke every now and then. Make fun of yourself. Laugh at yourself. It helps everyone, including you.

Alternatively, when it's time to have a difficult conversation, do you make them comfortable in an uncomfortable situation, or do you yell and scream at them until they're on the verge of tears? We all are human, and we all make mistakes. A mentor of mine says it all of the time: "The day that I have a perfect day is the day that I'll expect you to have one as well." Remember, even in times of discipline or corrective action, be nice and just be human."[11]

Dr. Griffin inspires us through this thought-provoking conclusion:

You are a leader. You are the example. People look to you for direction, for inspiration, for guidance, caring, and something to believe in. Provide it all and be the leader because when it all comes down, it ain't if, it's how they remember you.

Final Thoughts

This chapter, "Perception Versus Reality: How Leaders Inspire," addresses several areas of discussion for leaders to know and understand. Inspiration comes from how leaders lead and is attributable to behaviors, mannerisms, and attitudes that others observe and experience while in our presence.

In chapter two, we learned that generational differences do not necessarily cause division if we take the time to understand our similarities and listen to one another. To this end, since millennials outnumber the other generations in the workplace at the present time, a renewed focus on how they operate, communicate, process information, and want to be treated will help us to be a positive influence in their lives. The 2021 Global Leadership Forecast provides relevant data to keep us focused on the journey of effectively leading this generation.

The talent shortage, while impacted by the coronavirus pandemic, is a direct result of the expectations of the millennial and Gen X generations. Leaders must pause to analyze the statistics and trends. Leaders that choose to align with their expectations, desires, and perceptions will aid in developing, maintaining, and sustaining personal and professional relationships.

Lastly, the question, "How will you be remembered?" is a meaningful and thought-provoking question for all leaders. Workers don't leave the organization; they leave people (leadership). As Paul teaches young Timothy in 2 Timothy 3:16–17, we will be remembered as we inspire others through our instruction, conviction, correction, and training as a means for their growth and development.

STUDY QUESTIONS and DISCUSSION

Perception Versus Reality: How Leaders Inspire

1. How do you tap into potential in others?

    _____

    _____

    _____

    _____

    _____

2. What steps will you take to inspire others to greatness?

    _____

    _____

    _____

    _____

    _____

3. Identify three areas of growth that you need in order to position others for success.

    _____

    _____

    _____

    _____

    _____

4. How will you move your team from talking about inspiration to execution?

_____

5. Does your style of leadership model the desired outcomes that you seek for others?

_____

[1] "Latest Corporate Crisis: Only 11% of Surveyed Companies Have a Strong Leadership Bench," by Edward Segal, May 19, 2021, and "Leadership Transitions Report 2021," Development Dimensions International, Inc., 2021.
[2] "The Talent Shortage: How Did We Get Here and What Can We do About It?" Portico Consulting LLC, by Victoria Fuehrer, June 15, 2021.
[3] Market Watch – Economic Report, by Jeffrey Bartash, June 8, 2021.
[4] Ibid.
[5] Ibid.
[6] www.daxx.com
[7] U.S. Census Bureau.
[8] Ibid.
[9] Bridgeworks.
[10] "Who Changes Majors?" by Doug Lederman, December 8, 2017.
[11] "Leadership Lessons: How Will They Remember You?" Dr. David Griffin reminds officers that the people they lead seek not only direction but inspiration and caring. By Dr. David Griffin, June 14, 2021.

PART TWO:
Servant Leadership: Leverage for the Workplace

❧

We have different gifts, according to the grace given to each of us. If your gift is prophesying, then prophesy in accordance with your faith; if it is serving, then serve; if it is teaching, then teach; if it is to encourage, then give encouragement; if it is giving, then give generously; **if it is to lead, do it diligently;** *if it is to show mercy, do it cheerfully. Love must be sincere. Hate what is evil; cling to what is good. Be devoted to one another in love. Honor one another above yourselves. Never be lacking in zeal, but keep your spiritual fervor, serving the Lord. Be joyful in hope, patient in affliction, faithful in prayer. Share with the Lord's people who are in need. Practice hospitality.*

— Romans 12:6–13 (NIV)

4.
Frontline Leaders Want Role Models

AS A LEADER, YOU ATTRACT WHO YOU ARE,
NOT WHO YOU WANT. LEAD BY EXAMPLE,
AND SHOW PEOPLE THE WAY.

*Accept my teachings and learn from me, because I am gentle
and humble in spirit, and you will find rest for your lives.*

— Matthew 11:29 (NCV)

*We're living through real paradigm shifts in our culture, so now is
the time to change any behavior or practices that need changing.*

— Cynthia (Cynt) Marshall
Chief Executive Officer, Dallas Mavericks (NBA)

I vividly remember several leaders who were outstanding examples and wonderful role models for me and my fellow colleagues at the beginning of my federal government career. These were phenomenal men and women whose hearts and minds were focused on us as the next generation of leaders in the workplace.

For starters, Mr. Delma Hughes, Director and Program Manager of the Defense Logistics Agency Centralized Intern Development Program at the former Defense Personnel Support Center (DPSC) in Philadelphia, PA, was the first leader I met as I embarked upon this exciting journey. Mr. Hughes was instrumental in ensuring that the twenty-five interns from across the United States, most of whom were one year or less out of college, would have a memorable experience. He was responsible for creating curriculum for our classroom study as well as serving as the coordinator for our on-the-job training for our various assignments while assigned to the DPSC. Mr. Hughes was a well-groomed, well-mannered, tall, and handsome gentleman who was always well dressed and set the tone for how we should present ourselves as professionals and future leaders. Another leader who comes to mind is Mrs. Catherine Ward. Mrs. Ward was my first supervisor as I embarked upon my full-time career in this program at DPSC. She was poised, confident, professional, knowledgeable, empathetic, and compassionate with her varied leadership style. She was seasoned in her tenure with the federal government but willingly took me under her wing and openly shared with me, through words and action, how to conduct myself and how to handle the day-to-day activities I would be entrusted to lead. What an extraordinary experience as I began the process of learning my profession during this first year of the intern program.

Transitioning from Philadelphia, I began the journey of the next leg of this assignment at the Defense Contract Administrative Services Plant Representative Office at the IBM Corporation, Manassas, VA. While there, I met Commander Robert Gustavus, United

States Navy, and Mr. Robert White, Director. Both gentlemen, one military and one civilian, were stellar leaders in a relatively small organization of fifty men and women whose job was to support a Fortune 100 company. Under their leadership, I had an opportunity to learn, grow, develop, and mature in my role as a contract administrator with the responsibility of managing four major contracts on behalf of the federal government. Commander Gustavus and Mr. White were the epitome of professionalism, acumen, attention to detail, and subject matter expertise, and they excelled at creating an outstanding organization of fairness and equity for all frontline leaders to observe, embrace, and follow.

My initial experience under outstanding leaders during my first two years in the workplace still resonates with me. Mr. Hughes, Mrs. Ward, Commander Gustavus, and Mr. White showed me how and why leadership is so important, and from these humble beginnings, I was able to embark upon a thirty-four-year career. I remain thankful to each of them for their excellence in leadership.

Frontline leaders are perhaps the most excited group of leaders to enter their new positions, with vigor, high energy, and great anticipation. It's a new adventure filled with hope, positivity, and unmatched enthusiasm. In an *Inc.* magazine article titled, "3 Questions Newly Hired Leaders Should Ask to Understand What Their Workplace Is Really Like," dated December 8, 2021, Marcel Schwantes, Founder and Chief Human Officer, Leadership from the Core,[1] encourages frontline leaders to ask the following questions to quickly reveal the company culture as you enter your new role:

1. *What do the most successful leaders here care about most?* Identifying the answer to this question is perhaps the single fastest way to figure out what an organization's culture is like. If you know what gets rewarded by the people at the top, you will know what drives the culture.

2. *When people here fail, what's typically the cause?* This one can be a little bit more uncomfortable to ask, but it can lead to crucial insights. People usually fail for one of two reasons: Either they fail to achieve business results or they fail to achieve results in a culturally acceptable way. Employees probably value their culture, and therefore you should move a tad more slowly and observe it carefully.

3. *What's an early mistake people in similar roles make, and how can I avoid it?* Did the person before you burn out quickly? Did another leader rock the boat too much when stepping into a tightly knit team? How a company defines what a mistake is will reveal a lot about its culture. Learning about the specific situations that led to previous failures will help you decide how to assimilate—and how not to.

A crucial factor to understand as you enter a new leadership role is your organization's culture. Culture is what people and organizations care about. Misalignment to culture is one of the biggest reasons new leaders fail. Unfortunately, cultures are notoriously difficult to decipher.

Inherent to each of these three questions is a sense of generosity. That is, how tenured leaders respond to each question as we consider those who seek our mentorship, guidance, and direction has a direct correlation to our gratitude and appreciation to welcome you into the fold. It is a mutually beneficial approach that is regularly mentioned in Scripture (2 Corinthians 9:11, 13).

Table 1. Reflections on Generosity

Reflections on Generosity
Proverbs 22:9 – The generous will themselves be blessed, for they share their food with the poor.
Romans 12:13 – Share with the Lord's people who are in need. Practice hospitality.
Hebrews 13:16 – Do not forget to do good and to share with others, for with such sacrifices God is pleased.
2 Corinthians 9:6 – Whoever sows sparingly will also reap sparingly, and whoever sows generously will also reap generously.
1 Timothy 6:18–19 – Be rich in good deeds…be generous and willing to share. In this way [you] will lay up treasure for [yourselves] as a firm foundation for the coming age.
Proverbs 11:25 – A generous person will prosper; whoever refreshes others will be refreshed.
1 John 3:17 – If anyone has material possessions and sees a brother or sister in need but has no pity on them, how can the love of God be in that person?

While our leadership styles vary, let's not sacrifice our collective concern and desire for others to excel at what they are gifted to accomplish while at work. Generosity is one of many ways to send clear messages that we delight in their presence in our organization and on our team and that their contributions will be valued.

Frameworks & Culture

As a frontline leader seeking answers to the three questions about your organization's culture, your next step in this process is to understand the importance of having frameworks for understanding the culture that you are entering. Frameworks for understanding the culture you're entering include the following:

» Competitive versus Collaborative
» Humble versus Self-Promoting
» Traditional versus Innovative
» People Emphasis versus Results Emphasis

Table 2. Frameworks & Culture

Framework	Culture
Competitive versus Collaborative	In a competitive culture, individualistic high achievers get rewarded. In a collaborative culture, people who work well in teams tend to thrive, and good teams are rewarded together.
Humble versus Self-Promoting	In a humble culture, leaders are quick to distribute credit to others and are willing to admit mistakes. In a self-promoting culture, people focus on communicating their achievements and are quick to take credit when they can.

Traditional versus Innovative	In a traditional culture, the people who play within the lines are admired. There's a resistance to change, even if it might achieve better results. In an innovative culture, ideas are rewarded. Employees are encouraged to try new things.
People Emphasis versus Results Emphasis	In organizations with a people emphasis, how things are done matters as much as, or even more than, what the outcomes are. These supportive cultures value personal growth and skill development. In a results-first organization, you would be committing a cultural faux pas if you took an accommodating approach to a poor performer.

Assessing your culture correctly and assimilating to its norms are both crucial to succeeding in your new role—especially when you are still making an expression, building credibility, and strengthening your internal connections.[2]

Understanding The Boss

In 2013 one hundred companies participated in one of the first studies by ROI Communication benchmarking how well bosses were fulfilling their critical communication role. Unsurprisingly to those of us who had been paying attention to the problem, the study revealed some rather alarming findings:

> » Slightly fewer than half of the companies surveyed rated their managers as effective in their communication leadership roles.
> » Seventy percent of bosses did not understand the expectations of their role in communication.
> » Only 23% of companies defined communication competencies for all people managers.
> » Only 33% of leaders and managers received communication training.
> » Just 24% were held accountable in performance reviews for communication and leadership effectiveness.
> » A mere 33% explained company issues to their teams.

Presuming, as most experts do, that leadership and communication are codependent, these are appalling outcomes. In subsequent annual studies by ROI Communication, the numbers have not substantially improved. As leaders, we are responsible for the entire communication process.[3]

Based upon Roger D'Aprix's research on this topic, there is a remedy, but it is far from easy. What companies—and communicators—can do requires a radical rebalancing of corporate priorities. They include the following, just to name a few:

> » Valuing of professional leadership at the front line, where it matters
> » A generous investment in the training, development, and accountability of leaders at every level

» Recognizing that a company's true competitive advantage is the talent and well-being of its workforce.

It also requires cultural and structural change:

» Agreement that work is essential to our personal sense of worth and dignity, with an emphasis on employee retention versus mindless automation and employee downsizing to increase shareholder value.

» Match best leadership practices with precise selection criteria to ensure the best boss candidates.

» Senior leadership can establish deliberate initiatives to create a culture of leadership and to make their companies people centric.

In two case studies, Pfizer and QVC led by example through industry best practices to demonstrate a commitment to frontline leadership through a series of bold moves. In 2012 Pfizer's leadership launched a five-part initiative entitled "Creating an Ownership Culture," abbreviated simply to the acronym OWNIT!

The five parts of the initiative were based on the meaning of that acronym:

» **O**wn the Business – Seize opportunities to think differently and be accountable.

» **W**in in the marketplace – Support long-term and aligned strategies.

» **N**o jerks – This refers to boss behavior with the further admonition that there be no corrosive, self-serving, or mean boss behavior. The goal is for the company to be people oriented as a prime cultural value.

» **I**mpacting results – Deliver on commitments with integrity.
» **T**rust – Trust in one another and company relationships.

The other example is QVC, the home shopping channel. Under the leadership of CEO and President Mike George, the company engaged in a longstanding initiative to educate employees fully on vision, mission, and strategy. The fundamental notion is that everyone in QVC must be a leader, with leaders of leaders at the top of the organization, leaders of people in the middle, and "leaders of oneself" as the primary agent and talent in serving customer needs. The entire culture of leadership initiative is fully supported by human resources and other staff functions to keep the company focused on necessary changes.

Clearly there's a need for much more effective frontline leadership. Historically, this leadership level has been given the least attention and development. In fact, research from Gallup claims that senior leaders make the wrong choice in selecting boss/manager candidates 82% of the time. In their annual reports on the "State of the American Workplace," they assert that for American business alone, the estimated cost of this neglect exceeds $350 billion annually.[4]

Developing Your Network

Welcome to your new place! Now the work begins to make it a safe place for you and your colleagues.

Your network can be defined as a fabric or structure of cords or wires that cross at regular intervals and are knotted or secured at the crossings. It is an interconnected or interrelated chain, group. or system.[5] As you develop your network throughout your career, think of it as an ongoing and never-ending support system that you can rely upon as you make decisions and solve problems. Observe Diagram 1 below as a tool, and envision you as the center piece:

Diagram 1. My Network

Ask yourself a set of three open-ended questions, and respond in kind to each of the four steps in building your network. In doing so, you create an action plan that aligns with your specific goals and objectives as you consider both tactical and short-term as well as strategic and long-term aspirations.

Step 1 – Identify your five "critical" relationships.

> » Which key leaders in my organizations do I need to know on a personal and professional level?

» Which key leaders in my organization need to know me on a personal and professional level?

» From whom and what can I learn at my level to give the most impact?

Step 2 – Seek and identify your "build" relationships.

» I want to add value to my organization, but how do I do that?

» What organizations should I join to gain greater insights into the mission, vision, and core values of my company?

» What senior-level leaders have a reputation of wanting to mentor frontline leaders?

Step 3 – Designate those that will be a part of your "collaborative" network.

» My colleagues and peers should be my biggest allies. Who are they, and how should I make their acquaintance?

» What is the best day and time to have a recurring meeting with a trusted colleague?

» How can I help two to three peers achieve their goals?

Step 4 – Pursue those that you will develop into leaders.

» I want to pour into the lives of future leaders. Who in the human resources department do I contact to proactively identify men and women that want a mentor?

» What topics of discussion work best for the next generation of leaders?

» How do I balance my time and resources to be available to serve others?

It will be tough to endure the challenges and complexities of leading people without a well-defined and carefully built network that you can tap into from time to time when needed. It is an essential ingredient to your journey in this sought-after domain in the workplace. Navigate with caution, and reach out for help. It is available, but it takes action on your part to use your network wisely. Serve others and you are being served.

Final Thoughts

In this chapter, we explored several principles and strategies that will aid our frontline leaders as they matriculate into their respective roles of responsibility. These leaders are looking for role models that will show them the way, lead the way, and help them navigate the way. In addition to the words that we communicate, they want to emulate observable mannerisms and behaviors.

During this pivotal time in the lives of these leaders, we should assist them in understanding what the workplace is really like and their new culture through frameworks, how to manage their boss effectively and diligently, and how to build a powerful and protective network.

In doing so, these leaders are well on their way to a prosperous and successful career.

STUDY QUESTIONS and DISCUSSION

Frontline Leaders Want Role Models

1. What is the importance of leading by example?

\
\
\
\
\

2. Do you agree that leaders are role models? Why or why not?

\
\
\
\
\

3. Leadership is a spiritual gift. Why do you believe that God gifted some of His children this way?

\
\
\
\

4. What are the top two skills needed for a frontline leader?

_____

_____

_____

_____

_____

5. How does servant leadership align with your personal and professional development?

_____

_____

_____

_____

_____

[1] *Inc.* magazine, "3 Questions Newly Hired Leaders Should Ask to Understand What Their Workplace Is Really Like," dated December 8, 2021, Marcel Schwantes, Founder and Chief Human Officer, Leadership from the Core

[2] ROI Communication, 2013

[3] "The Boss Issue: The Cost of Neglecting Frontline Leadership Development," www.iabc.com, by Roger D'Aprix, April 1, 2020

[4] Merriam-Webster Dictionary, 2022, Merriam-Webster, Inc.

[5] Leading Effectively Through Change and Conflict, "Navigate Your Leadership Journey," December 8, 2014, www.leadership.opm.gov

5.
Mid-Level Leaders Seek Answers

DEVELOPING THE NEXT GENERATION OF LEADERS
IS PERHAPS THE HIGHEST CALLING FOR A LEADER.

*"Ask, and it will be given to you; seek, and you will find;
knock, and it will be opened to you. For everyone who
asks receives, and he who seeks finds, and to him
who knocks it will be opened."*

– Matthew 7:7–8 (NKJV)

Approximately fourteen years into my career with the federal government, I had an urge for something bigger and better. I had a strong desire for a position with increased responsibility, visibility, and accountability. So I diligently sought opportunities and mentors to help me achieve this goal. In 1995 I sought acceptance into a premier leadership development program for high-potential mid-level employees in the federal government called the Executive Potential Program. The duration of this leadership program would be twelve months and would offer multiple opportunities for a myriad of developmental assignments, classroom training, growth, development, and learning from senior executives that would be the prerequisite to move into senior leadership positions.

To this end, I applied to this program and presented a multi-page application to my immediate supervisor. She was already on the record as someone who supported my personal and professional goals. Upon her review and consideration, she approved the package and then passed it on to her supervisor for review. By the time that the process was completed, my application package for consideration for the Executive Potential Program was read and considered by five levels of leaders within my government agency. I learned later that no other mid-level leader within our organization had ever applied for this leadership development program. In the end, it was approved, but I did create an uproar because there were other leaders within our organization that did not think it was fair for me to be approved for the program without going through some type of formal process. A few of the leaders argued that the process was not fair and equitable.

Months later, it was revealed that since I was the first employee to apply for the program—and approved—a formal application process would result. I am extremely grateful for the support that I received from the five different levels of leaders who chose to review and consider my application. T. his leadership development program proved to be a difference maker in my career but equally important, it sent a very clear message that I had great support from the senior leadership team within the agency. I was at a pivotal moment in my career as I sought answers to many, many questions as a mid-level leader. I know that I would love the opportunity to one day serve as a senior leader but did not know how.

Upon graduation from the Executive Potential Program, I was promoted to a regional chief procurement officer position in New York, New York, and I was well on my way to learning what it took to work within the cadre of my fellow mid-level as well as senior leaders within the region and across the country. It proved to be a wonderful experience.

Let the Journey Begin

Strengths – Weaknesses – Opportunities – Threats (SWOT)

Movement into a new phase of our careers and leadership journey should begin with an in-depth review and understanding of our current state of readiness. There are many tools to help us look in the mirror for a time of self-reflection and self- assessment but perhaps none better than a SWOT analysis, created by Albert Humphrey, who developed the approach at the Stanford Research Institute back in the 1960s and early 1970s.

A SWOT analysis is a tool for conducting a quick assessment of the situation. It is very useful for creating understanding when (1) addressing conflict or (2) beginning to determine courses of action for leading change. It can be used individually or with a team.

Table 1. SWOT Analysis

Internal	External
Strengths:	Opportunities:
Weaknesses:	Threats:

Internal Influences – Examples include attributes and characteristics that we currently do or do not possess. These present opportunities to develop, improve, and continue to mature.

Strengths:

- » Communication
- » Vision
- » Professionalism
- » Tact
- » Drive
- » Self-motivation

Weaknesses:

- » Listening
- » Empathy
- » Developing others
- » Completing projects timely
- » Giving direction
- » Presentation skills

External Influences – Examples include situations and circumstances out of our control, such as reorganizations, new boss, new teammates, revised/updated company vision, recently elected government officials, or a career change. In each instance, it's how we react to what is happening around us that reveals our level of maturity.

Opportunities:

- » Restructuring
- » Rewritten policy
- » Updated human resources directives
- » U.S. Presidential Order No. 14035 – Diversity, Equity, Inclusion and Accessibility
- » Newly appointed director

Threats:

- » New Board of Directors
- » Economic instability
- » U.S. Supreme Court decisions
- » Weather conditions
- » Shift in priorities by senior leadership

Utilizing this tool is a step forward in the lives of all leaders. At the mid-level especially, new responsibility, visibility, and accountability expose your vulnerabilities as well as strengths early in your work role. Preparedness is key.

Be Action-Oriented

Selena Wilson is the Chief Executive Officer of the East Oakland Youth Development Center. In her article titled "A True Leader Actively Does These 3 Things Every Day" in *Leadership Now* (February 11, 2022), she reflects on what she learned from the organization's former chief executive about leadership and development. They are:

1. *Create opportunities for others to lead.* Strong leaders do not wait for others to rise to the occasion. They create opportunities that show people the potential that lies within them.

2. *Set the bar high, and offer support.* Setting expectations is essential to the success of any organization. In fact, a leader's failure to set expectations often frustrates team members and undermines the outcomes. As leaders, we must establish and communicate clear and achievable expectations for those we serve, but we must not stop there. True leaders not only set expectations but also provide support and guidance to ensure that others have the necessary tools to succeed.

3. *Cultivate an ecosystem where everyone thrives.* Leadership is a team effort. No successful leader will ever tell you that they accomplished great things on their own.

We are encouraged to actively do these three things every day.[1]

Mid-level leaders soon discover that although many people seek to avoid work or work as little as possible, the Bible presents, in general, a positive view of work. It views work, in itself, as a good thing and as pleasing to God (2 Timothy 3:17).

The U.S. Department of Labor's December 2021 jobs report showed the country's labor force participation rate at only 61.9%—down from 63.4% in February 2020, before the COVID-19 lockdowns shuttered businesses, resulting in 18 million layoffs by April 2020. Yet in December 2020, the number of people not working—who, when surveyed, said they wanted a job but weren't looking—was 5.7 million.

Has something happened to America's work ethic?

The Bible has much to say about the value of work—from creation, through the rise and fall of civilizations, and to the fulfillment of Christ's Great Commission. As God's image bearers, Christ-followers are called to glorify their Lord and Savior in their work and service to others.

Here are five reasons why God gives us productive work to do:

1. *The satisfaction that comes from productive work and "earned success."* God created humans in such a way that we gain deep joy and satisfaction from doing meaningful, productive work. Economist Arthur Brooks summarizes academic research showing that, surprisingly, the most satisfying economic activity for human beings is not earning great amounts of money but rather what he calls "earned success," that is, having a specific responsibility and then doing

good work to fulfill that responsibility in whatever career or field one chooses. This echoes the biblical theme that we experience deep satisfaction from God's recognition that we have been faithful servants and have accomplished the work that He gave us to do. This ultimately will be affirmed when God says to us, "Well done, good and faithful servant. You have been faithful over a little; I will set you over much. Enter into the joy of your master" (Matthew 25:21).

2. *The privilege of creating something new.* When we work to make things, we create something that did not exist in the world before we made it. This is a faint imitation of God's own creative activity. It also reflects other attributes of God, such as His wisdom, knowledge, strength, and patience. God gives us the privilege of imitating Him in various ways, for Scripture tells us, "Be imitators of God, as beloved children" (Ephesians 5:1).

3. *The privilege of creating value.* It's not just that we create products. It is that these products have value to us and others. Whether we bake a loaf of bread or assemble a new computer, these things have greater value than the raw materials they possess. Therefore, in doing productive work, we add to the total value of the useful things that exist in the world for the benefit of mankind.

4. *The privilege of supporting ourselves.* Paul told the Thessalonian Christians to "work with your hands...so that you may walk properly before outsiders and be dependent on no one" (1 Thessalonians 4:11–12). Our natural sense of human dignity is reinforced when we can support ourselves

and no longer depend on our parents or others. Productive work gives people a new sense of self-respect, and it glorifies God by giving a faint imitation of God's own attribute of independence. Not having productive work soon brings frustration due to not being able to do what God made human beings to do: to be engaged in useful, productive work and thereby support themselves.

5. *Individuality.* God created human beings with vast differences in skills, preferences, and inclinations for the types of work we enjoy and want to focus on. This diversity among human beings is a gift that leads us to specialize in different kinds of work, and it makes the human race thousands of times more productive than if we all had to produce everything we needed for ourselves (as do animals when they have to find their own food). Therefore, because of specialization, we are able to fulfill God's command to subdue the earth (Genesis 1:28) and make useful products from it in a much more extensive way that we otherwise could.

"But if our work actually results in a benefit to other people, then we should understand our work as one way of showing love to others."[2]

Data Reveals a Call for Help

On May 26, 2022, the Equal Employment Opportunity Commission (EEOC) issued its Fiscal Year (FY) 2019 report titled "Federal Workforce Report." EEOC is a leading federal government agency whose mission is "to prevent and remedy unlawful employment discrimination and advance equal opportunity for all in the workplace." The wonderful work of the commission continues in the hopes of realizing their vision: "Respectful and inclusive workplaces with equal employment opportunity for all."

The EEOC has the authority to investigate charges of discrimination against employers who are covered by the law. Their role in an investigation is to fairly and accurately assess the allegations in the charge and then make a finding. If they find that discrimination has occurred, they will try to settle the charge. If they are not successful, they have the authority to file a lawsuit to protect the rights of individuals and the interests of the public and to litigate a small percentage of these cases. When deciding to file a lawsuit, the EEOC considers several factors, such as the strength of the evidence, the issues in the case, and the wider impact the lawsuit could have on the EEOC's efforts to combat workplace discrimination.

They also work to prevent discrimination before it occurs through outreach, education, and technical assistance programs.

The EEOC provides leadership and guidance to federal agencies on all aspects of the federal government's equal employment opportunity program. EEOC ensures federal agency and department compliance with EEOC regulations, provides technical assistance to federal agencies concerning Equal Employment Opportunity (EEO) complaint adjudication, monitors and evaluates federal agencies' affirmative employment programs, develops and distributes federal sector educational materials and conducts training for stakeholders, provides guidance and assistance to their Administrative Judges who conduct hearings on EEO complaints, and adjudicates appeals from administrative decisions made by federal agencies on EEO complaints.

Mid-level leaders should review and consider the key findings contained in the "Federal Workforce Report" for FY 2019. The headline is "People with Targeted Disabilities Show Gains; Retaliation Tops Complaint Bases." An executive summary is highlighted here:

The report revealed some encouraging news about people with targeted disabilities in the federal sector. The overall participation rate of this population rose from 1.05% in FY 2003 to 1.80% in FY 2019—a 71% gain. This was driven by increases in the participation rates of individuals with serious difficulty hearing, serious difficulty seeing, and significant psychiatric disorders, the EEOC said.

The report showed that the federal government mirrors the private sector in one key respect: Of the 15,070 formal discrimination complaints filed in FY 2019, the basis most frequently alleged was reprisal/retaliation (7,487 charges). Retaliation has also been the most common basis for discrimination charges in the private sector for many years now. The second and third most common bases in the federal sector are physical disability (4,252 complaints) and age (4,382) discrimination.

Carlton Hadden, director of the EEOC's Office of Federal Operations, said, "We continue to see slow but steady progress in the federal sector with regard to key indicators of the EEOC's mission to foster inclusiveness and eliminate discrimination."

Among other significant findings:

>> There were 36,348 counselings completed during FY 2019, with an alternative dispute resolution (ADR) offer rate of

87.06%, an ADR acceptance rate of 54.10%, and an ADR resolution rate of 66.50%.

» EEOC investigators spent, on average, 227 days to complete investigations during FY 2019, up 20% from the previous year. The average cost of an investigation was $4,288.

» The average monetary pre-complaint settlement was $4,023 per settlement, with a total government-wide settlement pay-out of roughly $3.1 million, down from $3.6 million in FY 2018.

» The total number of findings of discrimination, including Administrative Judge decisions and final agency decisions, increased from 139 in FY 2018 to 175 in FY 2019—over a 25% increase.

» In FY 2019, the monetary benefits obtained through settlements and awarded for findings of discrimination at the complaint stage, including Administrative Judge decisions and final agency decisions, amounted to over $53 million, a 1.7% increase since FY 2018.

» 61.4% of agencies reported that the immediate supervisor of the EEO director was the agency head.

The annual report informs and advises the President and Congress on the state of EEO throughout the federal government.[3]

Leaders are learners. In that spirit, a leader takes the time to understand what is happening within the bowels of their government agency, corporation, non-profit, church, or academic institution to help make things better for the workforce. The data is available. Seek and find then offer a hand.

It's All About the People

In a very insightful article titled "Why Leadership Development Should Be at the Core of Your People Strategy in 2022," on Forbes.com, May 2, 2022, by Kelly Kubicek, Forbes Councils Member, the author shares several principles on how to understand and develop a people strategy in your organization. Kelly is the co-founder and CEO of Fulcrum HR Consulting.

People strategy represents a company's principal plan concerning its human capital. It corresponds to the methods business and HR leaders use to attract job seekers, grow leaders, retain workers, build connections, and inspire the workforce to drive innovation. But most of all, the people strategy encourages the C-suite (senior executives) and stakeholders to agree on crucial issues and decisions regarding people. After all, people are the most significant aspect of every company.

Moreover, an efficient people strategy drives business success, productivity, high-performing teams, and employee engagement and loyalty. It serves as a road map highlighting the path a company should take compared to its current, future, and potential workforce. For instance, business strategy is external and focuses on products, services, target audience, and customers. On the other hand, people strategy shows how a company can provide a better employee lifecycle and build a tight-knit bond with workers.

Although people strategy has many similarities with HR strategy, the latter focuses more on administrative rather than strategic tasks. These two often intertwine, but classic HR departments foster a fixed mindset that allows them to address contractual problems and challenging regulations. As a result, others often see these professionals as gatekeepers. People strategists have close connections with every department due to depending on collaboration to increase human capital.

In a nutshell, here are the top four benefits of an efficient people strategy:

» High-performing talent
» Cohesive leadership
» A stable and healthy company culture
» Increased diversity, equity, and inclusion

Why Should Leadership Teams Be the Core of Your People Strategy?

Cohesive leadership teams drive the company vision and guide people through challenging times. Businesses can only thrive if decision-makers agree on critical issues and lead by example. Otherwise, the work environment becomes disorganized, and managers might struggle without having a sense of direction. That also affects employees as they become aware something is off, causing them to lose a sense of belonging.

Moreover, stable leadership and healthy company culture are among the pillars of an efficient people strategy. That is even more important in times of uncertainty and crisis after switching to remote work, when employees have missed out on team interaction and office culture.

Because of that, HR teams should first develop resilient and agile leadership teams that can foster a purpose-driven culture, empower people, and help employees navigate challenging moments. They should also have a growth mindset and find opportunities within hardships. That allows them to respond to complex situations proactively instead of merely reacting. Without that approach, leadership teams could fail to shape the company's future and make employees a part of that.

The only way to have a resilient company, shared vision, and alignment on business goals and people strategy is to develop future leaders. Because of that, HR needs to establish comprehensive training and opportunities that encourage employees to strive for managerial positions and take the initiative. For example, they should identify skills gaps, provide upskilling and reskilling, and foster internal mobility. Workers should know that they can advance in the company and participate in shaping the company's vision.

People are the most significant and efficient asset of every company. They shape its future, generate new ideas, and reach long-term goals. Because of that, it should be a priority to nurture employees' development, invest in leadership teams, and foster workplace connections.[4]

Final Thoughts

In this chapter, we explored the pivotal transformation into the role of a mid-level leader. With it comes a tremendous amount of responsibility, accountability, and visibility. Your success as a frontline leader has positioned you for a higher level and more complex challenges. A key takeaway is finding a well-developed network of like-minded colleagues and peers that you can lean on during times of need.

We started with a reminder that developing the next generation of leaders is perhaps the highest calling for a leader. I learned about this truth during my progression into the middle leadership ranks through the unwavering support that I received from five levels of leaders when I applied to the Executive Potential Program. At that time, no one else in the entire organization of 123 employees had ever applied to any leadership development program, although the federal government offers several opportunities every year. The most senior-ranking executive, who had the final vote on my application package, said, "I approved this application because Kevin had the foresight and proactive confidence to do so even though we do not have a written process that governs how to select interested candidates for leadership development programs." I was, and remain today, thoroughly impressed with such a bold and supportive response from him.

Become familiar with your strengths, weaknesses, opportunities, and threats as a part of your day-to-day development. Acknowledge the current state of your organization in terms of how the workforce is treated by its leadership team. For the federal government, the data is verified through the EEOC, but such measurable statistics are also available through a plethora of sources for churches, corporations, non-profits, and academic institutions. As you study the data, act on it on behalf of those that do not have a voice.

Lastly, it's all about the people! Ensure that they are taken care of through your organization's resources, tools, training, and developmental assignments. They represent the future, so help them to feel included, valued, and appreciated. It makes a difference.

STUDY QUESTIONS and DISCUSSION

Mid-Level Leaders Seek Answers

1. What steps have you taken to develop others?

_____

_____

_____

_____

_____

2. Do you embrace the idea that leaders are learners? Why?

_____

_____

_____

_____

_____

3. List one example of how you serve others as a role model.

_____

_____

_____

_____

_____

4. The next generation of leaders is positioned for greatness. How will you ensure that this happens?

_____

_____

_____

_____

_____

5. Mid-level leaders can sometimes feel stuck in place. List at least two methods that you can employ to assist them.

_____

_____

_____

_____

_____

[1] FastCompany.com, "A True Leader Actively Does These 3 Things Every Day," by Selena Wilson, Chief Executive Officer of the East Oakland Youth Development Center, February 11, 2022.

[2] Decision Magazine, "How God Values Our Jobs: We Are Called to Work as Unto the Lord," by Wayne Gruden, February 2022, pages 11–13.

[3] www.eeoc.gov

[4] Forbes.com, "Why Leadership Development Should Be at the Core of Your People Strategy in 2022," May 2, 2022, by Kelly Kubicek, Forbes Councils Member.

6.
Senior-Level Leaders Require Reinforcement

LEADERS ARE LEARNERS. DO NOT ALLOW
YOUR THIRST TO LEARN TO BE QUENCHED.

"None of us are as smart as all of us."

— Ken Blanchard, Don Carew, and Eunice Parisi-Carew,
The One Minute Manager® Builds High Performing Teams

As I teach, share, facilitate, and instruct on the topic of leadership across the nation and the world, I intentionally remind all my students that "leaders are learners." It's a memorable phrase that I use frequently. The important takeaway from this simple yet profound truth is for us to never allow our thirst to be quenched or our hunger to be satisfied when it comes to learning. It is an ongoing, continual, and recurring process that should become a habit through repeated patterns and practices.

As a senior-level leader in the federal government as well as in ministry, I have learned over many years that one of the best things a senior leader can offer to those that we are entrusted to lead is character, integrity, and respect. These are my top three core values. When we make a conscious choice to exercise these characteristics and attributes on a regular basis, it sends a very clear message to everyone in the organization that they have our support and that we are more than willing to serve them. Senior leaders have a heightened level of responsibility to ensure that the workplace is safe, comfortable, and conducive for learning, growth, and developing others. Therefore, by the time we reach senior-level positions, all of the prerequisites required should be in place and should be mastered. This level of leadership has the responsibility to ensure the welfare and well-being of all employees while, in parallel, taking care of customers and stakeholders. In doing so, we have the necessary ingredients for the organization to thrive and for every employee to feel that they can bring their creativity and innovation into the workplace.

The Descriptive Leadership Development Landscape

A profound shift in the human experience is at work. We are at a pivotal moment in the history of leadership and leadership development. Why? Because we are in the middle of a radical transformation of the human experience at work.

First and foremost, the COVID-19 pandemic has forced a shift to remote work in many companies. As a result, leaders are struggling to connect with their teams more than ever, especially when there is a lot of change and emotional upheaval.

Second, there has been a deep change in the role of purpose in business. It has always been a fundamental truth that the purpose of business is to make money. In late 2019 the business roundtable and association of Chief Executive Officers from two hundred of America's most prominent companies declared that the fundamental purpose of business is as follows:

» Deliver value to customers
» Invest in their employees
» Deal fairly and ethically with suppliers
» Support the communities in which they work

Coming in at number five on their list was what most assumed would be at the top: generating long-term value for shareholders.

60% of frontline leaders say they have never received any training or preparation for a leadership role.

While this statement caught the attention of many observers, it did not come as a complete shock. After all, this reordering of priorities reflects the culmination of trends that have been building for some time. In a world that is highly transparent, people want to know the companies they buy from, partner with, and work for are positively impacting the community.

This sense of ethics and community purpose was called into question even more during the social unrest during 2020. Organizations are expected to do good in the world and value diversity and inclusion for all employees.

And that creates a major shift for leadership development.

New Demands on (Senior) Leadership Development

It's no surprise that these trends have had a deep impact on leadership development. Today's corporate leaders are called on to do more than manage work. They need to be masters of emotional intelligence, expert coaches, and engaging motivators. They must help people see the purpose in their work and show them clear paths for growth, all while delivering business results.

It is critical that every company begin to reevaluate not only which skills are most necessary but how they can develop these skills in their (senior) leaders. Doing so will require organizations to navigate a growing maze of learning and development options. But it also requires an understanding of the state of modern leadership.

Leadership Development Redesigned

The shifts in (senior) leadership require new ways of thinking about leadership development and new ways to address them.

Table 1: Development Dimensions International's 5 Best Practices

1. Context Matters in Leadership Development	2. Design "Leader-First" Experiences	3. Variety Is the Spice of Learning	4. Don't Leave Development to Chance	5. Learn to Perform
Leaders will have different development needs depending upon their context.	*Technology isn't changing the landscape for leadership development. The expectations and needs of today's leaders are.*	*Trying to pick the best learning method is like trying to pick the best ingredient in a recipe.*	*The foundations are the foundations for a reason.*	*It's less about learning and more about performing.*

How can leaders acquire new skills and knowledge?

Leadership is learnership. Select the best option based on the outcomes and results you need.

Table 2. Options for New Skills and Knowledge

What's in Your Mix?	This Option Works Best to:
In-Person Classroom	» Build awareness and skills. » Practice skills with other leaders. » Learn from the experience of others.
Micro Courses	» Raise awareness. » Enhance knowledge with related skills or topics. » Address immediate and unplanned needs.
Web-Based Training	» Gain knowledge on skills or topics. » Test understanding and mastery. » Establish a common knowledge base before a classroom experience.
Virtual Classroom	» Build awareness and skills. » Practice skills with other leaders. » Manage travel costs.

How can leaders apply and sustain learning?

Plan purposeful ways for leaders to continuously learn and grow in their careers.

Table 3. Applying and Sustaining Learning

What's in Your Mix?	Examples
Coaching	» Coaching from manager, peers, or an external coach » Skills based or problem based
Development Tools	» Job aids » Planners » Templates
Feedback	» Formal or informal » From immediate manager, peers, or key stakeholders
Games and Simulations	» Group competition in the classroom » Individual games or sims to test and practice skills » Gamification programs
Manager Support	» Overview of program content » Development plan template » Application tools
Virtual Reality	» Empathy-generating scenarios » Skill-building scenarios

1

Vision

Vision is defined as the act or power of anticipating that which will or may come to be. It can be characterized as the prophetic vision or the vision of an entrepreneur.[2] With it, leaders can flourish. Without it, leaders become stuck in the past or present, missing out on future opportunities to grow and thrive.

Below is a representation of how senior leaders can inspire and encourage others to catch the vision, embrace it, align with it, and, ultimately, achieve it. It begins with the leader and continues in a clockwise motion.

Diagram 1. Vision

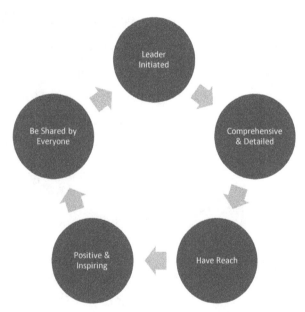

Leader Initiated – Credibility comes from the top down.

» Have you demonstrated over an extended period that you are credible? Do people believe in you and your leadership?

Comprehensive & Detailed – Everyone needs to know where they fit in and how they are going to contribute.

» How well do you communicate the vision, task, assignment, or project? Are you clear, concise, and to the point?

Have Reach – It must be worth the effort.

» Does the vision include a heightened level of awareness about the desired outcome? Do you help others "see" what's ahead?

Positive & Inspiring – People must believe in the change or initiative to commit to it.

» Does the vision uplift the individual contributors, the team, and the organization? Have you asked the team how they feel about their participation?

Be Shared by Everyone – Everyone needs to be on board to bring the vision to light.

» Contributions to the cause is key. Have you gained buy-in from most of the team?[3]

In Scripture, Habakkuk 2:1–2 says, "I will stand upon my watch, and set me upon the tower, and will watch to see what he will say unto me, and what I shall answer when I am reproved. And the LORD answered me, and said, Write the vision, and make it plain upon tables, that he may run that readeth it." Since leadership is a spiritual gift (Romans 12: 6–8), vision comes from God. Note that Habakkuk continues in verse 3, relative to the outcome from the vision that comes from God into the hearts of leaders, "For the vision is yet for an appointed time, but at the end it shall speak, and not lie; though it tarry, wait for it; because it will surely come, it will not tarry."

Feedback

See your blind spots, and discover how you come across. Feedback offers many benefits. It is essential that senior-level leaders give effective feedback as well as receive timely feedback. It is a necessary practice if we are to improve, develop, and go beyond our current limits. One of the more meaningful outcomes of feedback is that it helps us to see our blind spots and to discover how we come across to others.

There is always a gap between the self we think we present and the way others see us. We may not recognize ourselves in others' feedback, even when everyone else would agree that it's the conventional wisdom about who we are and how we are. Why is there such a gap between our self-perception and others' stories about us? The good news is that the ways we are understood and misunderstood by others are amazingly systematic and predictable.

The Gap Map, developed by authors Douglas Stone and Sheila Heen, highlights the key elements that factor into the way we mean to be seen versus the way we are actually seen. Read from left to right, the Gap Map makes the cause of our blind spots visible.

Diagram 2. The Gap Map

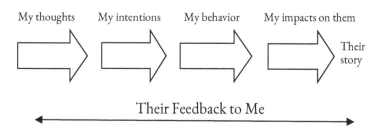

On the far left, we start with our own thoughts and feelings. From these, we formulate intentions: what we are trying to do and what we want to have happen. To achieve our intentions, we do and say things; we put behavior out into the world. These behaviors have an impact on others, and based on this impact, others develop a story about our intentions and character. They then offer some version of these perceptions to us as feedback. By the time others are describing you—to you—the figure they are describing may bear only a vague resemblance to the "you" you know. We flinch, we squint, and we shake our heads. We do not recognize ourselves.

Somewhere in the game of telephone, messages get garbled. By looking more closely at how information moves across the map, we can pinpoint where and why.

What Helps Us with Our Blind Spots?

A blind spot is something we don't see about ourselves that others do see. We each have our own particular items in our blind spot basket, but there are some blind spots we all share. If we circle (on our map in Diagram 1 above) the things I am aware of and the things you are aware of, it turns out that my behavior is in *your* awareness and mostly *not* in my awareness.

Let's start with what doesn't help. You can't see yourself more clearly just by looking harder. Here's why: When you do take a good, hard look, what you'll see is that you don't have any blind spots and that the feedback is wrong. You will wonder about the cause of this wrong feedback, and your mind will slide into an explanation about the ulterior motives or personality disorders of those that gave you the feedback. We have the same Gap Map reaction to them as they do to use, just in reverse. We know that we are upset by wrong feedback and assume that others are giving it to us intentionally, which means they must have an agenda or that something is seriously wrong with them.

Use Your Reaction as a Blind-Spot Alert

Thoughts like the above are so systematic that you can actually put them to good use. Instead of dismissing the feedback or the person giving it to you, use these thoughts as a blind-spot alert. When you notice yourself wondering, *What was their agenda?* and *What's wrong with them?*, make sure your next thought is *I wonder if this feedback is sitting in my blind spot?*

Lastly, consider three blind spot amplifiers because our blind spots are their hot spots. There are three dynamics that amplify the gap between how we see ourselves and how others see us. They are interrelated, but each is worth examining on its own.

> » Amplifier 1: Emotional Math – Emotions play a huge role in the gap between how others see us and how we assume we are seen. We subtract certain emotions from the equation: "That emotion is not really who I am." But others count it double: "That emotion is *exactly* who you are."

» Amplifier 2: Situation Versus Character – Emotional math is really a subset of a larger dynamic. When something goes wrong and I am part of it, I will tend to attribute my actions to the situation; you will tend to attribute my actions to my character.[4]

» Amplifier 3: The third amplifier has already been hinted at on the Gap Map: We judge ourselves by our intentions (Arrow 2), while others judge us by our impacts (Arrow 4). Given that even good intentions can result in negative impacts, this contributes to the gap in the story you tell about me versus the story I know is "true."

Look for Patterns

Our usual response to upsetting feedback is to reach for other feedback that contradicts it to protect ourselves. You say I'm self-absorbed? Then how come I won the community service award last year? You think I interrupt? Let me stop you right there...because I practically had to sit on my hands last week during your inane presentation.

Instead of whipping your contradictory feedback, take a breath and look for consistent feedback—consistent in two ways. First, consider to what extent you are each describing the same behavior but interpreting it differently (as the table below illustrates). Others may be misunderstanding you (shy versus aloof), or you may be unaware of your impacts (outgoing versus overbearing). The feedback is not initially what you expect, but once it's reinterpreted, you can at least identify the behavior being discussed.

Here's a second way to look for consistencies: Ask yourself, *When have I heard this before?* Is this the first time you've gotten such feedback, or have you heard similar things from other people (or the same exact person) over the years? Patterns offer useful clues about blind spots. If your first grade teacher and your spouse both complained about your hygiene, it might be time to listen.

Table 4. Patterns

How I See Me	How Others See Me
Shy	Aloof
Upbeat	Phony
Spontaneous	Flaky
Truth Teller	Nasty
Passionate	Emotional
Smart	Arrogant
High Standards	Hypercritical
Outgoing	Overbearing
Quirky	Annoying

5

Reinforce Versus Redirect

Senior-level leaders provide and receive feedback regularly to show appreciation, to hold others accountable, and for the purpose of development. Below is an illustration showing the benefits of feedback on both ends of the spectrum, which maintains a proper balance. Leaders should reinforce outstanding work and redirect subpar work. Employees that are contributing their best to the team and organization receive reinforcement, that is, "thank you for a job well done," whereas employees that require more development, coaching, mentoring, and support are redirected for the purpose of improving their performance.

Diagram 3. Reinforce Versus Redirect

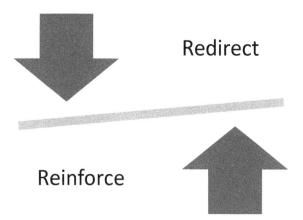

To maintain a healthy balance within the organization, each employee should be the recipient of both formal and informal feedback that will redirect their current efforts as skills need development. Simultaneously, employees that are tapping into their potential and doing good work on behalf of the team and organization require reinforcement so that they never feel that their talents are being taken for granted. Examples include:

Reinforce – to show appreciation

- » "Thank you for a job well done today."
- » "I really appreciate your contributions to the team."
- » "Great presentation this morning."

» "Your suggestion to adopt the new HR policy has been a tremendous benefit for our group."

» "The customer says you explained our mission in simple terms that they could understand."

Redirect – for the purpose of positive development

» "Your voice did not project in this afternoon's briefing. I have some good suggestions to help you for your next one."

» "I caught a typographical error on page four of your memo. I have an outstanding editor that I can recommend."

» "Your performance appraisal produced a lower overall evaluation, but I have several great resources that you will find helpful for the next cycle."

Final Thoughts

Chapter 6 not only concludes Part 2 but it presents the senior leadership community with thoughts and ideas for leverage in the workplace. These thoughts include the following:

» Be in the state of a continuous learner.

» Recognize and acknowledge the ever-changing leadership development landscape because a profound shift in the human experience is at work.

» Vision: The best leaders have it and communicate it in a manner that others can understand and embrace it. The prophet Habakkuk reminds us of its important and the gravity of hearing from God.

» Feedback is a multi-faceted component in the workplace. Some crave it, while others dread the thought. Use the appropriate means of feedback based upon your leadership style. Be authentic and genuine in your approach to achieve the best results. Reinforce the positive, and redirect for the purpose of improvement and development.

This chapter is a reminder that regardless of our current and past accomplishments, there is a wealth of information that we can learn and apply. Once we do so, we then pass it on to those whom we are entrusted to lead. My personal challenge for all senior-level leaders is to read at least one book every month. Just as technology is regularly updated and revised so are leadership development strategies and principles. Stay fresh, and be mindful of the needs of others.

STUDY QUESTIONS and DISCUSSION

Senior-Level Leaders Require Reinforcement

1. Reinforcement and redirection for senior-level leaders are very important for their growth and development. What observations can you add to this statement?

    _____

    _____

    _____

    _____

    _____

2. Continuous learning is a sign of humility. What scripture reminds you of this truth?

    _____

    _____

    _____

    _____

    _____

3. Reading is fundamental and necessary. How many books do you read each month?

    _____

    _____

    _____

    _____

    _____

4. Coaching is one of many ways to reinforce the need to achieve at a high level, even as a senior leader. Have you hired a coach? Why or why not?

_____

_____

_____

_____

_____

5. Describe two ways that you will not allow your thirst to learn more ever to be quenched.

_____

_____

_____

_____

_____

---

[1] Development Dimensions International, Inc., 2020 www.ddiworld.com.

[2] Merriam-Webster Dictionary, 2022, Merriam-Webster, Inc.

[3] Joel Barker, Power of Vision

[4] This is known as the actor-observer asymmetry (Jones and Nisbett, 1971). The actor tends to attribute their behavior to the situation, while the observer tends to attribute the actor's behavior to the actor's character. A related concept is the fundamental attribution error (Lee Ross, 1967), which states that when we describe the behavior of others, we overemphasize character and underemphasize situation.

[5] *Thanks for the Feedback: The Science and Art of Receiving Feedback Well*, by Douglas Stone and Sheila Heen, Penguin Books, 2015, Chapter 4, pages 77, 78, 81, 86–88, 90, and 92.

PART THREE:

Servant Leadership: Moving Organizations Forward

Jesus replied, "Your mistake is that you don't know the Scriptures, and you don't know the power of God."

— Matthew 22:29 (NLT)

7.
Grow Self

People fail to get along because they fear each other;
they fear each other because they don't know each other;
they don't know each other because they have not
communicated with each other.

— Reverend Dr. Martin Luther King, Jr.,
Winner of 1964 Nobel Peace Prize

Good leadership begins with self-awareness. The more we are in alignment with ourselves, the better positioned we are to serve and lead others. As frontline, mid-level, and senior-level leaders in our respective careers, questions arise that deserve well-intentioned answers. Often the answers come from within.

A thirst and an appetite to learn about our unique leadership styles, emotional intelligence, personality styles, behavioral styles, and conflict management styles puts us in a position to support others and develop them. As leaders, we must learn to become comfortable in our own skin and understand the value of looking in the mirror first for self-reflection and self-assessment (internal) before we look through the lens at others (external). This simple yet important practice helps every leader put into perspective what others may be dealing with and the various issues that confront us—and them—daily. In doing so, we can make the best decisions and solve problems with clear thinking. I am an advocate of the myriad of leadership assessments that are available in the marketplace because they offer insight to help leaders evaluate self and encourages feedback from others. It is a necessary and essential tool for the most effective leaders. We have a responsibility to grow self through reading, study, practice, and application throughout our leadership journeys and career progression. As we seek and get answers to our many questions, we become better prepared and equipped to lead others through the myriad of challenges that they face in their personal and professional lives.

Performance

If you want to know why people are not performing well, step up to the mirror and take a peek.[1]

How well are you performing? What do others say about your performance? Creating a plan of action and developing goals is a good step forward to obtain an honest answer to these questions. As you measure your progress and evaluate the necessary adjustments, consider the table below. Write down your desired outcome for development goal one and two for the three categories listed: review, plan, and initial.

1) Review: This is a self-assessment of your performance to date.

2) Plan: Solicit a coach to help shape your current performance, and practice developmental activities.

3) Initials: This is your accountability partner or mentor that will provide an honest assessment for the purpose of helping you to improve your performance.

Table 1. Measuring My Progress & Making Adjustments

Date		1st Developmental Goal	2nd Developmental Goal
Review	What is going well for me?		
	Where am I running into obstacles?		
Plan	What do I need to do more of?		
	What do I need to do less of or change?		
Initials	The person to whom I report progress		

2

The Principles of Self-Management

As a company grows, it also needs to grow its capacity to perform. However, investing in new equipment, technology, and buildings is not enough. A self-managed and accountable organization provides the underpinning required to develop flexible management techniques that grow with the firm. The best way for a company's formal leaders to create a culture of self-management and accountability is to demonstrate it themselves.

What is self-management, and who needs it?

Self-management is the ability and the will to act in the company's best interest in such a way that intrinsic motivation replaces any external consequences imposed to reward or punish performance. The fundamental principle is that intrinsic motivation is the path to performance excellence at all organizational levels. Self-management is appropriate for any position. Formal leaders in the executive suite need it just as much as frontline employees. The word "empowerment" is often used to help people increase their initiative and discretion. But this word, however well meaning, suggests that the hierarchy above grants power to the troops below. Formal leaders can influence but not control others' behaviors. Your influence will come by embracing the wisdom of Mahatma Gandhi when he said, "Be the change you want to see in the world."

Core principles

Five core principles form the foundation of a culture of self-management. Living these principles will enable employees and leaders to find the path to greater self- management in whatever position they hold. While not listed in any particular order of importance, each principle is a tool that can be added to your toolbox. They are:

Principle 1: I work for the customer, not my supervisor. An organization exists to create value for its customers. The value the customer receives must be greater than the cost it provides. A noble mission statement, the greatest technology, or a marketing strategy are not substitutes for the customer's perception of value.

Principle 2: I manage my own performance. When employees and leaders accept the responsibility to manage their performance, they take the primary responsibility to establish clear goals, report on work progress, initiate discussions on both performance breakdowns and breakthroughs, and make recommendations for future actions. Self-management does not eliminate the supervisor. In fact, self-management provides an opportunity for formal leaders to spend more time with high value organizational improvement activities.

Principle 3: My supervisor and I are partners in performance. Self-management is not a solitary activity. An employee and her supervisor are partners in performance and servicing customers. Healthy partnerships are synergistic and respectful and have a win–win orientation.

Principal 4: I am loyal to the truth. The price of self-management is to be loyal to the truth and for employees to provide accurate and timely information to the customer and the supervisor on their commitments and performance. There are three elements to personal accountability:

1. Make clear commitments.
2. Initiate and communicate results on a timely basis.
3. Own the consequences without excuses or blame, always focusing forward on improved performance. Being loyal to the truth is the essence of a high-integrity person.

<u>Principle 5</u>: I am a lifelong learner. While organizations need to improve their processes and ability to perform, each leader has the same challenge. Although it is good for the company to provide opportunities for professional growth, ultimately each individual needs to lead the way. Employees investing time in professional growth is as important as investing money for future financial health. This increases value to the company and strengthens employees and leaders' quality of life.[3]

True leadership is not about a position or title. As a

leader, the most important earthly relationship you can cultivate is your relationship with yourself.[4]

Assessments

Companies should be putting people in charge that demonstrate competence, humility, and integrity. If you're responsible for assessing leadership candidates, you should work on your ability to distinguish between confidence and competence. Fortunately, you can use scientifically valid assessments to measure the traits you want (or don't want) in your leaders, to take self-assessments, and to then measure their responses against their leadership style, performance, and effectiveness. The resulting data will help identify patterns that characterize good and bad leaders at your company.

Of course, this practice will take time and effort, and many organizations won't want to invest those resources. But vetting candidates for leadership roles will pay dividends down the line.[5]

Why Assessments?

Data trumps hunches and prevents bias from corrupting important decisions. Throughout the latter half of the twentieth century, Fortune 500s relied on behavioral and cognitive assessments to inform all aspects of their personnel decisions—from an employee's initial selection and training to their team role and eventual promotion. These paper-based assessments had to be individually calculated by a highly trained professional, making them too expensive for most organizations to afford. However, with the advancement of new computer technologies and algorithms, the cost of such assessments has dropped measurably, leveling the playing field for businesses of all sizes. Assessments offer the following benefits to better our leaders in government, corporations, churches, nonprofits, and academic institutions:

1. Improve Hiring and Selection. The right person in the right job is priceless.
2. Increase Sales. Teach your sales team powerful behavior profiling skills. Empower them to identify—to your organization's advantage—observable behaviors then adapt their selling style to fit the customer's buying style.

3. Improve Customer Service. Know in advance that your people believe in your organization and care about your customers.

4. Increase Productivity. Identify with scientific accuracy the strengths and shortcomings of each employee. Create observable action plans, from the data, that maximize your organization's talent.

5. Reduce Employee Turnover. Ensure the best possible positional job "fit" for each new hire. Great fits mean higher retention rates.

6. Customize Employee Training. One size fits ONE, not all. Learn how each person learns best, and get them back to productivity sooner.

7. Model Team Building. Know who fits with whom in advance. Create your teams based on compatible skills and traits, not just generic ideas of balance.[6]

People prediction is risky business. So much is at stake, and there are so many variables involved in getting it right, including environment, situation, relationships, relevancies, knowledge, skills, experience, education, and more.

Applying Assessment Science

After decades of work and research on how to assess the dimensions of people, Dr. Tony Alessandra and his team found these scientifically based assessments would provide the best foundational approach:

» **DISC:** The world's number one behavioral profiling tool

» **Motivators:** A measure of the Seven Universal Dimensions of Motivation that drive us all

» **Critical Thinking** (based on the Hartman Value Profile): A measure of critical thinking and processing ability, decision-making skills, and situational bias

» **Emotional Intelligence:** A measure of our EIQ to help users understand their own emotions and the way in which emotions impact interactions with others

Other ways to use assessments not mentioned above can be found in Diagram 1.

Diagram 1. Best Ways to Use Assessments

Select better teams	Make managers better leaders	Improve employee coaching

Manage difficult team members	Provide managers and employees a common language

Better teams ➔ There is more to team success than just finding the best people for the team. Team success is often dependent on how the team members work together.

Better leaders ➔ Because there are no right or wrong answers to assessments, just different types, managers can become better leaders. Armed with this knowledge, managers can do more to motivate teams, communicate change, and delegate effectively.

<u>Improve employee coaching</u> ➔ When coaches understand the person they are working with, they can tailor their approach to maximize success.

<u>Manage difficult team members</u> ➔ Assessments can diagnose potential sources of workplace conflict. Prevention is the best approach.

<u>Common language</u> ➔ The language of the assessments can improve team communications.

Identifying and Exploring Behavioral Styles: DISC Assessment

Misunderstanding behavior is a disease that afflicts the human race. We are a society struggling in disagreements, false impressions, and misinterpretations about people's behavior. It's paralyzing when we consider how fundamentally important it is for people to live in shared communities and our basic need for human connection.

With eight billion unique individuals on the planet, a lack of understanding of human behavior should come as no surprise. The real wonder is how we communicate at all, much less understand one another's behavior and emotions.

The history of DISC theories, strategies, and tactics are not new. The idea of measuring and classifying temperatures into four categories has been around for a long time. While the language and descriptions have changed, the four primary types have a great deal of consistency over time. Here is a breakdown of how some of the foundations and language of DISC has evolved through the ages:

Table 2. DISC

	D	I	S	C
Hippocrates Humors – 400 BC	Choleric	Sanguine	Phlegmatic	Melancholic
Aristotle Elements – 350 BC	Air	Fire	Water	Earth
Carl Jung Functions – 1921	Extroverted / Thinking / Sensing	Extroverted / Feeling / Intuiting	Introverted / Feeling / Intuiting	Introverted / Thinking / Sensing
William Marston Primary Emotions – 1928	Dominance	Inducement	Submission	Compliance
Walter Clarke Vectors – 1940s	Aggressive	Sociable	Stable	Avoidant
Assessments 24x7 Behavioral Styles – 1970s	Dominance	Influence	Steadiness	Conscientiousness

DISC is a simple, practical, easy-to-remember, and universally applicable model of understanding needs-motivated, observable behavior and emotion. It combines awareness of nature (the inherent) and nurture (the learned) characteristics and reveals behavioral tendencies in natural and adapted styles.

D = Dominance: How people address problems and challenges

I = Influence: How people handle situations involving people and contacts

S = Steadiness: How people demonstrate pace and consistency

C = Conscientiousness: How people react to procedures and constraints

DISC measures the intensity of characteristics using scales of directions and openness (direct/indirect and guarded/open). It also looks at these through descriptors of pace and priority.

An Intro to Emotional IQ Styles: Emotional Intelligence (EIQ)

Emotional intelligence (EIQ) is a way of recognizing, understanding, and choosing how we think, feel, and act. It shapes our understanding of ourselves (intrapersonal) and our interactions with others (interpersonal). Intrapersonal recognition and management deals with recognizing, acknowledging, and working with our own emotions and expression. Interpersonal recognition and management examines relationships, empathy, connection, and social skills. EIQ is all about exploring how we perceive, access, generate, understand, express, and regulate our emotions and the emotions of others in ways that work to further our effectiveness and connections rather than undermine them.

The importance of EIQ can easily be measured in personal and professional success in many ways:

» Communication

» Decision-Making

» Leadership

» Sales

» Teamwork and Team Performance

» Productivity

» Relationship Satisfaction

» Customer Service

» Conflict Management

» Overall Effectiveness.

EIQ is measured through two competencies, *recognition* and *management*, with two perspectives, the *self* and *social*, resulting in four quotients.

Table 3. EIQ

	Self – Intrapersonal	Social – Interpersonal
Recognition	**Self-Recognition** » Self-confidence » Awareness of emotions » Recognizing cause and effect in emotion » Paying attention to changes in emotional states	**Social Recognition** » Empathy » Picking up the moods of others » Caring what others are going through » Reading both verbal and nonverbal signals

Management	Self-Management	Social Management
	» Creating goals and direction	» Sustaining quality relationships
	» Discipline and self-control	» Handling conflict effectively
	» Upholding personal standards	» Leadership and influence
	» Flexibility and adaptability	» Collaboration, cooperation, and teamwork
	» Optimism	» Effective interaction
	» Motivation and initiative	

There are several benefits to understanding EIQ for individuals and organizations. Our self-awareness blossoms with each new collection of information, and this insight gives us the opportunity to see how we connect with and express our own emotions and how we navigate the emotions of others effectively and appropriately to build stronger relationships. Having mutually beneficial, mutually respectful, and connected relationships is required to reach personal and professional effectiveness, and EIQ is a foundational viewpoint to navigate those interactions with expertise.[7]

Final Thoughts

As we begin our journey through Part 3, this chapter reiterates a key theme that great leadership begins with self. That is, know yourself.

In Scripture, Jesus said, "Your mistake is that you don't know the Scriptures, and you don't know the power of God" (Matthew 22:29, NLT). Contrary to what we hear from the plethora of motivational speakers on the lucrative speakers circuit across our nation and the world—raking in millions of dollars annually from the organizations, conventions, conferences, and summits that are willing to pay them—every leadership principle and strategy known to man comes from the Bible. And as already mentioned, leadership is a spiritual gift (from God, Romans 12:6–8). Studying the Bible is a discipline that causes us to examine self.

How and why we measure performance aligns with self-management. Table 1 is an aid to assist us with our performance that needs to be adjusted. It helps us see deficiencies and allows for revisions as necessary. In this spirit, the five core principles of self-management form the foundation of a culture of self-management. Living these principles will enable employees and leaders to find the path to greater self-management in whatever position they hold. True leadership is not about a position or title. As a leader, the most important earthly relationship you can cultivate is your relationship with yourself.

Assessments are yet another way to assess and analyze ourselves, personally and professionally. Fortunately, you can use scientifically valid assessments to measure the traits you want (or don't want) in your leaders and self by taking self-assessments and then measuring their responses against their leadership style, performance, and effectiveness. To this end, we examined the "why" for assessments (Diagram 1), the DISC (Table 2 history), and the EIQ (Table 3) and their unique significance. Use these tools as a way to continually improve, grow, and mature through-out your career progression and leadership journey.

STUDY QUESTIONS and DISCUSSION

Grow Self

1. The steps that I will take to increase my self-awareness are:

_____

_____

_____

_____

_____

2. My emotional intelligence results reveal the following about me.

_____

_____

_____

_____

3. My effectiveness as a leader has a direct correlation to my time of preparation. How many hours per week do I spend preparing myself to lead others?

_____

_____

_____

_____

4. My personality and behavior style is:

_____

_____

_____

_____

_____

5. My personal and profession balance is a reflection of how I prioritize what's important. What areas of my life require imme-diate attention for better balance?

_____

_____

_____

_____

_____

[1] *The Heart of a Leader: Insights on the Art of Influence*, Ken Blanchard,1999
[2] Leading Effectively Through Change and Conflict, Navigate Your Leadership Journey, www.leadership.opm.gov
[3] "True Leadership and the Principles of Self-Management," by Michael Coulbourne, *Talent Development* (TD) Magazine, May 2019, pages 68–71.
[4] Ken Blanchard and Terry Waghorn, *Mission Impossible*
[5] Harvard Business Review Management Tip of the Week, June 7, 2022, "Stop Promoting Incompetent Leaders"
[6] 24x7 Assessments, www.assessments24x7.com
[7] *What Makes Humans Tick: Exploring the Best Validated Assessments*, by Brandon Parker, Jennifer Larsen, MAED, MSP, MBA, and Tony Alessandra, Ph.D. Indie Books International, 2021, Chapters 1, 2, 3, and 8.

8.
Grow the Team

T-E-A-M = Together – Everyone – Achieves – More

What makes networking work is that it sets up win–win situations in which all parties involved get to take something home. Networking is a sharing process. Until you understand that, you won't have much of a network.

— Earl G. Graves, Jr.,
Former Chief Executive of Black Enterprise

For many years, I have intentionally helped people understand the dynamics of a team. Team literally means **T**ogether **E**veryone **A**chieves **M**ore.

All leaders have the responsibility to bring individual talents, gifts, knowledge, and abilities into the workplace. In parallel, we also have a heightened level of responsibility to ensure that our giftedness complements the mission, vision, and core values of the organization in general as well as the team specifically. Effective teams operate at their best when the individual contributors make a conscious choice to come together as one: to share the responsibility to work on a given project, respond with the right attitude, solve problems, and make decisions. Along our leadership journeys, we collectively determine to place the value of the team ahead of ourselves as individual contributors (Philippians 2:4). When we do so, everyone shares in the credit that has been earned. Equally important, there is a balance with how well the organization performs and how well the team can execute. When we achieve

> *My dream for a better world is leaders who are inspired, authentic, moving purposefully toward missions that matter to create a better world for all.*
>
> *– Rev. Dr. Martin Luther King, Jr.*

together, it keeps everyone on the team motivated, inspired, and encouraged. At the end of the day, that is the goal that we are looking to achieve.

Team Dynamics

The future of work aligns with the key to managing in this era. It is all about putting trust in your people. Rolls Royce North America Chief Executive Officer Tom Bell has led the aerospace and defense supplier to adopt more flexible policies, and it's paying off. Washington *Post* columnist Danielle Abril shares in her article about what Bell is doing to put trust in their people.

Chief Executive Bell says the COVID-19 pandemic transformed the way he thinks about work. It is no longer a place but an activity. Bell relied on his team and his people to help with an $8 million redesign of the company's Indianapolis office, which opened in May 2022. He also learned that his team of skilled workers could digitally show how the Rolls Royce engine would integrate in the

U. S. Air Force B52 aircraft all while working remotely. The model ultimately landed the company a $2.6 billion contract with a major corporate conglomerate.

Belle shared his vision of how work is evolving at Rolls Royce North America, which employs about six thousand workers. Bell answered several questions in Abril's article, but I would like to highlight just three.

Question: How are you thinking about flexibility for workers whose jobs require them to be in person?

Answer: *If you are a manufacturing engineer, much of your job is out of the factory on the floor talking to mechanics and helping us build products, but that doesn't mean every day you necessarily have to be there. You have a cadre of people who can rotate in and out. You have people who can be on remote calls. We have all learned to trust video. So our mechanical and manufacturing engineers can look at problems even if they are at home. We are trying to think liberally about how we spread the wealth of hybrid work.*

Question: How did Rolls Royce invest in a new office given its flexible work policies?

Answer: *If you are tired of seeing people in 2D, you can come up and have a cup of coffee with somebody at the workplace. We have stopped assuming everybody is at work every day. We no longer have a desk for every person, and we certainly do not have a parking spot for every employee. We are no longer thinking you come to the workplace to work by yourself.*

Question: How has leadership training changed since the COVID-19 pandemic?

Answer: *We now have mandatory training which can be taken virtually. It is quintessentially the difference between management and leading. You can manage tactically easier when everybody is physically present. What is required in 2022, and beyond, is real leadership. You may not see people for some weeks, and that is okay. You need to embrace that and lead even more effectively rather than worrying about managing.*[1]

Employee Engagement in Everyday Actions and Behaviors

One-time initiatives don't suffice. *Talent Development* magazine columnist Christian Nardy reminds us that an engaged workforce does not arise from a single organizational role.

No longer do organizations and leaders doubt the business case for employee engagement; much evidence makes a strong case for it. Take Gallup's 2017 "State of the American Workplace Report," which includes compelling statistics on the competitive advantage organizations gain when employees are engaged, such as lower absenteeism and turnover and higher productivity, sales, customer metrics, and profitability. Companies now view employee engagement as a business imperative and spend significant amounts of money toward improving it. In fact, statistics cite organizations spending upward of a billion dollars annually on improving employee engagement.

Despite the dollars and resources companies put toward increasing engagement levels, not to mention all the literature written on the topic, Gallup reports that only one-third of the American workforce is engaged. This means that two-thirds of the workforce is not engaged or is actively disengaged. That shows that companies have not yet figured out how to drive a culture of engagement.

Employee Engagement Needs HR, Leaders, and Employees

Employee engagement is often looked at in one of three organizational roles—HR, leadership, or the employee—and so are the approaches to improve engagement levels. Countless articles discuss what leaders should do to improve engagement among their employees. Substantial literature exists on what programs and initiatives HR can enact.

An engaged workforce doesn't arise from a single organizational role; rather, it's a blend of all three. Engagement is a choice that manifests in the individual acts, attitudes, behaviors, and practices that occur in an organization every day. It arises from the combination of HR, leadership, and employees choosing engagement and showing up in ways that demonstrate their choice to engage. Engagement is not about expensive programs, grandiose gestures, or one-time events. In fact, it is an everyday occurrence that HR, leaders, and employees control, influence, and promote.

How to Really Drive Engagement

Everyone in an organization has a role to play. Each must collectively take ownership of engagement and do so in ways that best leverage their roles and influence in the organization. Here is a closer look at the different roles:

1) **HR's role:** HR plays an integral role in setting up the practices, structures, and environment that enable an engaged workforce. HR facilitates and reinforces the actions and behaviors that drive and organizes engagement. HR can, and should, leverage the role it plays in the employee lifecycle, starting at the beginning:
   » Hire the kinds of people that will own their engagement.
   » Offer supportive leadership and development.
   » Promote accountability.

2) **Leadership's role:** An organization's leaders are the vital sponsors, supporters, and models of engagement. Employees look to leadership for vision and direction, and they watch them, observing what they do and don't do as well as how they behave. That's why it is essential for leaders to act and behave in ways that promote and enable their employees' engagement:
   » Affirm employee actions and behaviors that contribute to engagement. Show appreciation to employees that act in ways that drive engagement, and make it known to others.
   » Actively manage the detractors. Avoid ignoring bad behavior; instead, make expectations clear, and hold the difficult conversations when needed to promote accountability.
   » Model actions and behaviors. It's critical that you demonstrate engagement because your employees notice your actions and behaviors.

3) **Individuals' role:** Individuals must take ownership of their engagement. They are also responsible for contributing to

the kind of environment they want to work in, which means they can, and should, take action to drive engagement on their teams and in their organizations:

» Frame engagement as within your control.
» Find out what engages you. When you take your organization's employee engagement survey, reflect on the results to understand your motivators and what it is you uniquely need to be engaged.
» Notice and act.

Employee engagement is not the result of expensive, flashy programs and initiatives. Rather, the collective responsibility in the everyday actions of an organization's HR, leadership, and employees drives high engagement levels.[2]

Together – Everyone – Achieves – More

Envision the diagram below to interpret and understand the value of working together toward a common cause:

Diagram 1. T-E-A-M

In this context, I use the triangle to emphasize the levels of importance. At the top of the triangle, leaders always acknowledge the importance of *everyone* on the team. In doing so, leaders send a message to their teams that every man and woman is valued, cared for, and respected and has something to add to the team. Each person's intellectual capital is solicited because their contributions are needed and desired.

In the middle of the triangle is the theme of *togetherness*. In Scripture, *together* is synonymous with oneness and unity (Psalm 133:1, Ephesians 4:3). Operating as one is the ultimate goal and the manifestation of a well-oiled machine. It demonstrates a spirit of cooperation and collaboration. Human behavior dictates that there will be some disagreements among the team from time to time. However, investment in relationship building paves the way for teammates to agree to disagree on selected ideas yet work together despite the varying perspectives.

On the left side of the triangle, *achieves* represents a collective movement toward, or accomplishment of, a desired outcome. In Chapter 6, I shared about the vision of the senior leader and strategies to effectively communicate it in a way that others would understand and align with it. The organizational goals, aspirations, and vision have a much better chance to be realized based upon team chemistry. A leader's charge must always include ways to develop our teams so that we can, and will, achieve more. Coach and mentor each member of the team to bring out their giftedness, talents, and skills. In doing so, they are encouraged and inspired to give their best each day and toward every project.

Lastly, on the right side of the triangle is *more*. I believe that every member of the team will show up for work with a desire to accomplish more than what is stated in their job description if they are treated with dignity and respect. They will indeed tap into their creativity and innovative thoughts if they know that their ideas, perspectives, and viewpoints are valued and recognized. There will be a renewed level of energy among the team to be all that they can be. Why? Because their leadership cares!

Final Thoughts

Chapter 8 introduces us to the concept of T-E-A-M. While I do not know the origins of "Together – Everyone – Achieves – More," it is a term that I use frequently as I facilitate leadership development training with frontline, mid-level, and senior-level leaders across multiple venues. At its core, the message intended is to heighten the level of awareness among all leaders that team chemistry is vital to the health of our teams and organizations. If the team is not in unison, we face BIG challenges.

Rolls Royce North America Chief Executive Officer Tom Bell answered a series of questions about how he led his company, his team, and his people to help with an $8 million redesign of the company's Indianapolis office, which opened in May 2022. When asked about how leadership training has changed, he responded, "We now have mandatory training which can be taken virtually. It is quintessentially the difference between management and leading. You can manage tactically easier when everybody is physically present. What is required in 2022, and beyond, is real leadership. You may not see people for some weeks, and that is okay. You need to embrace that and lead even more effectively rather than worrying about managing."

Employee engagement requires commitment and action from HR, leadership, and individuals. In doing so, again, it enhances the relationship and interaction among the team. To grow the team, leaders must engage with each member of the team in a manner that they feel, and know, their contributions are valued and appreciated.

STUDY QUESTIONS and DISCUSSION

Grow the Team

1. T-E-A-M: How do you define <u>T</u>ogether?

_____

_____

_____

_____

_____

2. T-E-A-M: How do you define <u>E</u>veryone?

_____

_____

_____

_____

_____

3. T-E-A-M: How do you define <u>A</u>chieves?

_____

_____

_____

_____

_____

4. T-E-A-M: How do you define <u>M</u>ore?

_____

_____

_____

_____

_____

5. Based upon how you individually defined each of the above, how do you define <u>T</u>-<u>E</u>-<u>A</u>-<u>M</u> in your own words?

_____

_____

_____

_____

_____

---

[1] *The future of work aligns with the key to managing in this era.* Washington *Post* newspaper, Page G2, July 17, 2022, by Danielle Abril.
[2] "Employee Engagement Is in Everyday Actions and Behaviors: One-Time Initiatives Don't Suffice," *Talent Development* magazine, May 2019 by Kristina Nardi, pages 44–47.

9.
Grow the Organization

"You are the salt of the earth. But if the salt loses its taste, it cannot be made salty again. Salt is useless if it loses its salty taste. It will be thrown out where people will just walk on it. You are the light that shines for the world to see. You are like a city built on a hill that cannot be hidden. People don't hide a lamp under a bowl. They put it on a lampstand. Then the light shines for everyone in the house. In the same way, you should be a light for other people. Live so that they will see the good things you do and praise your Father in heaven."

— Matthew 5:13–16 (ERV)

One of the most important ways that we can all work together to grow our organization is to align with its mission, vision, and core values. The mission statement shares why an organization exists, and the vision statement provides guidance and direction on how to fulfill the mission. The core values represent the organization's belief system and culture. It reflects the type of leaders and employees that the organization wants to recruit and retain over a period of time.

Organizations are similar in that respect. If your organization lists *unity* as a core value, then it's very important that every employee in the organization operates with that in mind. Another example of a core value for an organization is *respect*, that is, a visible demonstration of the utmost courtesy and appreciation that is extended to everyone in an equitable manner. This is how organizations show support for each employee to help them understand their worth and value. It is core to growing an organization. Your company, church, non-profit, academic institution, or government agency will not only attract the best and brightest talent but data also shows that you will retain them as well. Your colleagues in the HR department will thank you for exhibiting this key core value. If your organization continues to operate based upon the stated mission, vision, and core values, there's a high probability that your employees will prosper in their environment and also be retained, with fewer choosing to leave the organization. Senior leaders are responsible to make this happen.

What Employees Value

The Washington Post Magazine issues an annual report titled, "Top Workplaces."[1] As a part of the *Post*'s annual surveys, Energage measures what employees value most with respect to the workplace. The 2021 results were distinct from previous years. In the past, factors like pay, benefits, and career training played a prominent role in shaping employees' opinions. In 2021 employees were more likely to prioritize aspects of *belonging* and *stability*. Below, to gauge employees' priorities, Energage calculated how strongly each factor corelates with how employees rate their workplaces. The closer importance is to 100%, the more important the factor is. Listed below are the five highest and lowest factors:

Highest:

- » Strong Values – 90.6%
- » Attentive to Concerns – 88.1%
- » Helpfulness – 87.9%
- » Meaningfulness – 87.3%
- » Appreciation – 87.1%

Lowest:

- » Pay – 71.9%
- » Efficient Meetings – 71.0%
- » Formal Training – 70.7%
- » Loyalty – 66.1%
- » Benefits – 65.9%

Leadership: It's Never Been Tougher!

Leaders feel the impact of rapid change. Need proof? Consider these four major forces of change:

1. **Work:** Radically compressed

    Everything is being compressed: shorter work cycles, more complexity, experimentation, and rapid decision making. Business decisions that were once the domain of senior leaders are being pushed further down the organization.

2. **Structures:** Networked, virtual teams

    In more team-based, flat, networked organizations, the ability to get things done through others requires a different approach to traditional structures based on position power and authority. And as more of these teams work remotely, the ability to connect and influence virtually has become even more important.

3. **People:** Craving impact and purpose

    Employee expectations have changed dramatically. Employees want to know they are making a worthwhile contribution to the organization and society at large. They are looking for connection with their peers as they switch to remote teams.

4. **Leaders:** Constant transition

    Leaders themselves are in a constant state of transition, dealing with increasing uncertainty and ambiguity. As a result, what was once called "change leadership" is now simply leadership. Furthermore, many of them are doing it from a distance.[2]

Georgia-based Chick-fil-A receives about 40,000 "expressions of interest" each year from people hoping to operate one of its restaurants, according to company representative Carrie Kurlander: "The process of becoming a franchisee is very thorough and results in approximately 100 people being selected each year. We are very proud of the fact that those who are selected demonstrate the leadership ability and business acumen needed to own and operate our Chick-fil-A restaurants."[3]

Five Ways to Have Satisfied, Productive Employees

Creating an engaged workforce comes down to meeting the needs of employees at every level, from their basic needs to added benefits, which can be accomplished five ways. They are:

1. **Be compliant.**

   Employees need to feel safe, and that requires creating a business environment that's stable and legally compliant.

2. **Create a healthy culture.**

   Nothing can counteract a toxic culture; it will lead to attrition and affect your bottom line. Implement strong company values, and base your culture around them.

3. **Define purpose.**

   Instill your company's purpose. Do you have a solid mission? Ensure your employees have meaningful work and want to support you in reaching your mission.

4. **Recognize talent.**

   Teachers know that keeping children productive is all about getting creative with rewards. It is the same in the workplace; our need for recognition does not disappear as adults.

5. **Provide challenges.**

> To keep anyone interested in anything, there must be a challenge and a certain level of autonomy granted. Nothing kills productivity like boredom and micromanaging.

According to data from the Chief Learning Officer Business Intelligence Board, nearly 95% of learning organizations plan to either increase or maintain their current investment in leadership development. Meanwhile, TrainingIndustry.com says that leadership training is a $366 billion leadership industry, yet most of these leadership programs fail to create desired results.

With an estimated $166 billion annual spend on leadership development in the U.S. alone, organizations must transform these mission-critical programs to create real and lasting impact. *Chief Executive Officer* magazine surveyed 28,000 business leaders, who revealed that 74% of organizations use instructor-led leadership training and 63% use executive coaching to deliver training on the following top-rated leadership skills:

- » Improving Coaching Skills (a priority for 34% of respondents)
- » Communication (31%)
- » Employee Engagement (27%)
- » Strategic Planning and Business Acumen (21%)

So why aren't we better at delivering leadership programs that work?

That question is the focus of a McKinsey study that cites four critical areas for potential failure in leadership development training:

1. *Context conquers content.* While most leadership development training programs emphasize content, it's really context that matters most—having the clarity to offer the two or three things that matter most to the organization, not the forty-six things (or twenty-one irrefutable laws) that look like leadership.

2. *Too much reflection, not enough application.* In columnist Chris Westfall's book, *Leadership Language,* he asks the question, "Where does leadership really come from?" Without tying reflection to specific action, leadership initiatives are lost. Leadership comes from one place: inside of you. Leadership is a verb, discovered in action and demonstrated in application. Connect concepts to current events and tie ideas to action if you want a leadership program with real impact.

3. *Underestimating culture.* For consultants, coaches, and even in-house leadership training programs, preparing to battle the mindset within the organization can be the deepest challenge of all. Why? Because without receptivity, revelation can't occur. No leadership training program can truly succeed unless the organization is willing to look beyond these seven words: "That's the way we've always done things."

4. *What gets measured gets done.* If you want to see the success of a leader, don't look at her. Look at what her team is doing. If folks are leaving the organization or trying to find ways to work for someone else within it, there's a leadership disconnect. A successful leader is always building or retaining a powerful team. A successful leader creates more leaders.

High-growth organizations can maximize their investment in leadership development by focusing resources on what matters most: developing a customized leadership program based on their organization (not the consultant's). While experts might argue that the components of leadership are the same for all, leadership development doesn't work without a clear context and cultural understanding. Innovative companies understand that an investment in employee development requires connecting concepts to real work and that context is the most powerful predictor of leadership development success.[4]

In the June 2011 edition of the *Harvard Business Review*, authors Daniel Kahneman, Dan Lovallo, and Olivier Sibony wrote an informative article titled "The Big Idea: Before You Make That Big Decision." The theme is decision making. All leaders are encouraged to think through the process of making important decisions; hence, there is a series of questions that decision makers should ask themselves.

The authors developed a tool, based on a twelve- question checklist, that is intended to unearth defects in thinking—in other words, the cognitive biases of the teams making recommendations. The questions fall into three categories:

1) Questions the decision makers should ask themselves (questions 1–3)
2) Questions they should use to challenge the people proposing a course of action (questions 4–9)
3) Questions aimed at evaluating the proposal (questions 10–12)

It's important to know that because you cannot recognize your own biases, the individuals using this quality screen should be completely independent from the teams making the recommendations.

Table 1. Decision Making

Question	Thought
1. Is there any reason to suspect motivated errors, or errors driven by the self-interest of the recommending team?	Review the proposal with extra care, especially for over optimism.
2. Have the people making the recommendation fallen in love with it?	Rigorously apply all the quality controls on the checklist.
3. Were there dissenting opinions within the recommending team?	Solicit dissenting views, discreetly if necessary.
4. Could the diagnosis of the situation be overly influenced by salient analogies?	Ask for more analogies, and rigorously analyze their similarity to the current situation.
5. Have credible alternatives been considered?	Request additional options.
6. If you had to make this decision again in a year, what information would you want, and can you get more of it now?	Use checklists of the data needed for each kind of decision.

7. Do you know where the numbers came from?	Re-anchor with figures generated by other models or benchmarks, and request new analysis.
8. Can you see the halo effect?	Eliminate false inferences, and ask the team to seek additional comparable examples.
9. Are the people making the recommendation overly attached to past decisions?	Consider the issue as if you were a new CEO.
10. Is the based case overly optimistic?	Have the team build a case taking an outside view. Use war games.
11. Is the worst case bad enough?	Have the team conduct a pre-mortem. Imagine that the worst has happened, and develop a story about the causes.
12. Is the recommending team overly cautious?	Realign incentives to share responsibility for the risk or to remove risk.

The real challenge for executives that want to implement decision quality control is not time or cost. It is the need to build awareness that even highly experienced, superbly competent, and well-intentioned managers are fallible. Organizations need to realize that a disciplined decision-making process, not individual genius, is the key to a sound strategy. And they will have to create a culture of open debate in which such processes can flourish.[5]

Chief Human Resources Officers Struggle to Develop High-Quality Leadership Talent

More than one-third of HR leaders report struggling to develop effective senior leaders, and 45% struggle to develop effective mid-level leaders, according to Gartner, Inc. This is causing leadership bench instability, which is at an all-time high. Gartner research reveals that only 50% of approximately 2,800 surveyed leaders report they are well-equipped to lead their organization in the future.

"Chief Human Resources Officers (CHROs) are facing a number of emerging challenges, including unparalleled transparency and public pressure, increasing automation and digitalization changing the skills and competencies that are required for success, and new generations entering or leaving the workforce," said Sari Wilde, managing vice president in the Gartner HR practice. "In order to succeed, organizations must have a quality bench of leaders to continue driving business outcomes while leading the organization into the future."

To ensure a high-quality supply of leadership talent as well as bench strength and performance over time, organizations need to address five fundamental succession risks:

1) **Vacancies cause time-critical leadership responsibilities to be neglected.**

   Leading organizations recognize that no candidate may be a 100% match; instead, they focus on appointing a best-fit leader who demonstrates the fundamental skills required and pairing them with other leaders.

"Complementary leadership"—the intentional partnership between one leader and one or many leader partners to share leadership responsibilities based on complementary skill sets—enables organizations to fill critical skills gaps dynamically at speed and increase success. Gartner analysis showed organizations that use complementary leadership realized a 60% increase in team performance and a 40% increase in leaders' own performance.

2) Successors are often underdeveloped.

A recent Gartner survey showed that 81% of HR leaders cite lack of readiness as a top reason that a high-potential candidate was unable to fill leadership positions. Ensuring successors' preparedness is more difficult today than ever before due to increasingly shorter tenures at organizations, the rise of the gig economy, generational shifts in the workforce, and leadership roles that are constantly changing.

HR leaders need to ensure that their succession pipeline prepares candidates to execute against current as well as future business needs. Organizations can use scenario planning to identify likely future experiences that executives will need to address as the company evolves.

3) Succession planning based on existing roles misses the mark on future business needs.

The average organization has gone through five enterprise-wide changes in the past three years, and 73% of organizations expect more change initiatives ahead. However,

HR's succession management plans usually focus on existing leadership roles, failing to anticipate the leadership demands of evolving business priorities.

Progressive HR functions take a demand-driven approach to succession management that focuses on planning for future leadership needs. Planning for future leadership roles has almost double the impact on leadership bench strength as planning for existing leadership roles; however, only 15% of executives rate their HR team as effective in doing so.

4) A homogeneous pipeline can damage company culture and performance.

Many organizations still struggle with a lack of visible diversity across their leadership teams. Women held only about 27% of senior management roles in Standard & Poor's 500 companies in 2019. Racially and ethnically diverse employees account for only 13% of all senior leadership positions. A recent Gartner survey found that 88% of diversity and inclusion leaders identified "Promotions and/or Succession" as one of the talent processes most susceptible to bias.

As evidence continues to mount that diversity improves culture and performance, organizations have realized that a homogeneous succession pipeline poses significant risks to the bottom line. In 2019 more than half of heads of diversity and inclusion identified influencing succession planning efforts as a top priority. Decoupling the successor's role from the candidates themselves and considering the qualifications first and the candidate second is one tactic leading organizations are employing to diversify their pipelines.

5) Failure to provide transparency around succession management disengages employees.

Gartner research found that 71% of employees think employers should increase transparency. The companies that have responded and created a culture that allows for open conversations, awareness, and psychological safety see manifold benefits: more customer brand loyalty, more profits, and a superior employee experience.

The same principle holds true for succession; informing candidates of their potential next role can facilitate targeted development efforts, increase their readiness to take on that role, and ultimately drive business results. Organizations must consider their corporate culture and employee needs to determine how best to implement transparency around succession plans.[6]

The 25 Companies with the Highest Ranked Leadership Teams

There are very valuable lessons to be learned from studying the habits, attributes, and behaviors of seasoned C-suite executives in the marketplace. How do they grow their organizations? On July 22, 2020, Insider.com columnist Marguerite Ward shared her article titled "The 25 companies with the highest ranked leadership teams, according to employees."[7] While I admired every CEO mentioned in the article, I was especially enamored with a few worth mentioning that align with *Leadership with a Servant's Heart.* In descending order, along with a leadership quote, they are:

24. **Steve Hare** is the CEO of Sage, a management software company that develops and markets accounting software for small and medium-sized businesses.

Headquarters: Atlanta

Industry: Tech

Employee quote on the company's leadership: "I have never seen such clear communication and alignment from leadership on goals and direction."

22. **Alex Shootman** is the CEO of Workfront, which provides cloud-based work management solutions for enterprise teams.

Headquarters: Lehi, UT

Industry: Computer Software

Employee quote on the company's leadership: "An amazing vision for the company and transparent about where we are going. I have confidence every day I step into work."

20. **Tim Cook** is the CEO of Apple, a multinational corporation that designs, manufactures, and markets consumer electronics, personal computers, and software.

Headquarters: Cupertino, CA

Industry: Consumer Electronics

Employee quote on the company's leadership: "They are always looking for feedback on how to improve and often institute changes based upon feedback. No other company that I have ever worked for has done this same thing with such success."

18. **Wayne Peacock** is the CEO of USAA, a private Fortune 150 financial services company that provides banking, insurance, and investment to the military community.

Headquarters: San Antonio, TX

Industry: Banking

Employee quote on the company's leadership: "They understand that happy workers provide the best service to our customers."

16. **Mike Walsh** is the CEO of LexisNexis, a corporation providing computer-assisted legal research as well as business research and risk management services.

Headquarters: New York City

Industry: Information Technology & Services

Employee quote on the company's leadership: "My leadership team is responsive and supportive. I am given plenty of leeway and encouraged to make my own decisions."

13. **Chris Caldwell** is the CEO of Concentrix, a wholly owned subsidiary of SYNNEX Corporation, which is a technology-enabled global business services company specializing in customer engagement and improving business performance.

Headquarters: Fremont, CA

Industry: Outsourced Call Center

Employee quote on the company's leadership: "All leaders live the organizational culture. What stands out even more during these trying times is the complete commitment of the leadership team to the health and wellbeing of all staff. I am truly proud."

6. **Carlos Rodriguez** is the CEO of Automatic Data Processing (ADP), an American provider of human resources management software and services.

   Headquarters: Roseland, NJ

   Industry: Human Resources Software

   Employee quote on the company's leadership: "They genuinely care about the associates and clearly demonstrate it. They are very visible and involved."

3. **Sundar Pichai** is the CEO of Google, a multinational corporation that specializes in Internet-related services and products.

   Headquarters: Mountain View, CA

   Industry: Internet Cloud Computing

   Employee quote on the company's leadership: "Super humble, very caring, zero pride involved. Truly lovely and inspiring people in the leadership roles."

1. **Satya Nadella** is the CEO of Microsoft Corporation, an American multinational technology company that develops, manufactures, licenses, supports, and sells computer software, consumer electronics, personal computers, and related services.

Headquarters: Redmond, WA

Industry: Computer Software

Employee quote on the company's leadership: "They care about making decisions that will benefit everyone. Very trustworthy."

Notice the focus and attention on the leadership team and employees.

Final Thoughts

This chapter concludes Part 3 of the book. Moving organizations forward has a direct correlation to aligning with its mission, vision, and core values.

Growth for any organization begins with understanding what employees value. Energage's annual employee survey clearly shows that they value strong values, attention to concerns, helpfulness, meaningfulness, and appreciation. I believe that our human resources always valued these attributes from their leaders but are more vocal today than they were in the past. Thus, leadership has never been tougher, in part, because leaders are in constant transition. However, we did discover that there are five ways to have satisfied and productive employees: Be compliant, create a healthy culture, define purpose, recognize talent, and provide challenges for them.

With an annual spend of approximately $166 billion, *Chief Executive Officer* magazine shared, from a survey of 28,000 senior leaders, that the following top-rated leadership skills that need development are coaching skills, communication, employee engagement, and strategic planning and business acumen. As a reminder, what gets measured gets done. Good decisions are a result of asking twelve thought-provoking questions but also require careful thought.

Partnering with our chief human resources officers helps our organizations to develop high-quality leadership talent. To accomplish this goal, we explored five practices for review and consideration. In closing, I shared key quotes about several chief executives that represent the top 25 companies with the highest-ranked leadership teams. Notice the connection between senior leadership buy-in and employee contributions to the company's mission. This is how they grow their organizations.

Best Christian Workplaces

Since 2002, Best Christian Workplace Institute's (BCWI) Employee Engagement Survey has been completed by more than 340,000 employees from over 1,300 organizations in the U.S., Australia, Africa, Asia, Canada, Europe, and Central and South America. BCWI is an international, not-for-profit, research-based organizational development and human resources consulting firm with offices in Mercer Island, Washington, and London, Ontario. They equip and inspire Christian leaders to build an engaged, flourishing workplace. They believe that Christian-led workplaces can set the standard as the best, most effective places to work in the world. Founded in 2002, they exist to help measure and improve the health of organizations through surveys, the 360 Leadership Review process, and consulting services.

Their 2022 list of Best Christian Workplaces[8] organizations in the U.S., Canada, Thailand, Australia, Indonesia, and Zambia and includes a variety of faith-based nonprofits, churches, and Christian-owned businesses. These workplaces reported strong satisfaction with team dynamics, even during a season when external research reveals the prevalence of isolation and disconnection at work.

What's unique about organizations that are certified as Best Christian Workplaces? Employees at these workplaces affirm good teamwork and conflict resolution skills in their responses to the BCWI Employee Engagement Survey. Even in the face of lower satisfaction with compensation and benefits, employees find high levels of meaning and value in their work as their organizations achieve their goals.

Workplaces that are flourishing have leaders who are proactive rather than reactive in a changing environment. Chief Executive Jay Bransford underscores the importance of great leadership in influencing workplace culture:

> We live in a world of dynamic change—from changing global political and economic realities to cultural shifts in society. Effective leaders need to continuously take the pulse of their organizations to better understand the state of their flock and how best to support, attract, and retain top talent. No other factor impacts the performance of an organization to a greater extent than its culture. Therefore,

proactively assessing and developing a healthy culture is a strategic imperative for all leaders. BCWI is the expert in assessing the culture of Christian organizations—applying robust data and experienced, professional consultants to guide you along the road to flourishing.

To this end, the organizations that made the list are divided into the following ten categories:

» Churches
» Faith-Based Organizations
» Missions and Parachurch
» Academic Institutions / Christian Schools
» Camps / Conference Centers
» Christian-Owned Businesses
» Family Services
» Media
» Products and Services
» Rescue Missions

In the words of Bransford, "Proactively assessing and developing a healthy culture is a strategic imperative for all leaders." What steps will you take to create a culture that will ensure that your organization becomes a workplace of excellence?

STUDY QUESTIONS and DISCUSSION

Grow the Organization

1. Define mission.

_____

_____

_____

_____

_____

2. Define vision.

_____

_____

_____

_____

_____

3. What are the core values of your organization?

_____

_____

_____

_____

_____

4. Why is it important to know and align with your organization's mission, vision, and core values?

_____

_____

_____

_____

_____

5. Is your current organization fulfilling its mission, vision, and core values? Why or why not?

_____

_____

_____

_____

_____

---

[1] *Washington Post Magazine*, "Top Workplaces: The Great Return, What Employees Valued in 2021," June 18, 2021

[2] Dimensions Development International, 2020

[3] Washington *Post* newspaper, June 8, 2018.

[4] Forbes.com, "Leadership Development Is a $366B Industry: Here's Why Most Programs Don't Work," by Chris Westfall, June 20, 2019.

[5] *Harvard Business Review*, "The Big Idea: Before You Make That Big Decision," by Daniel Kahneman, Dan Lovallo, and Olivier Sibony, June 2011.

[6] Gartner Press Release, "Gartner Identifies the Top Five Succession Risks That Derail Organizations' Leadership Strategies: CHROs Struggle to Develop High-Quality Leadership Talent," January 16, 2020. www.gartner.com

[7] Insider.com. "The 25 companies with the highest ranked leadership teams, according to employees," by Marguerite Ward, July 22, 2020.

[8] Best Christian Workplaces Institute, "109 Organizations Honored as "Certified Best Christian Workplaces of 2022," Faith News Service Press Release, by Robert Wachter, Global Director of Marketing, www.faithnewsservice.com / www.bcwinstitute.org

Conclusion

"An individual has not started living until he can rise above the narrow confines of his individualistic concerns to the broader concerns of all humanity."

– Reverend Dr. Martin Luther King, Jr.

Leadership with a Servant's Heart: Leading in Your Workplace serves as a resource for you and your team during this time of unprecedented change and transformation in our respective workplaces. Leaders at all levels are challenged with a diverse set of situations and circumstances that require a new, fresh, and different set of skills. We are entrusted to lead people across four generations that have different needs, wants, expectations, and objectives when they show up. Do we quash their goals, aspirations, and dreams, or do we work closely with them to accentuate their creativity and ingenuity? Not once did I mention that it is easy, but it is achievable.

In the spirit of the book title, our **hearts** are the foundation for our lives and God's ultimate focus for years. We have been taught to look upon sin and to war against, struggle against, rebuke, and fight sin when we should have been taught to focus where God is focused: our **hearts**, where the real battle rages. Hence, reading and studying *Leadership with a Servant's Heart* is both a physical and spiritual introspection into your career progression and leadership journey since you began leading others, that is, being a servant leader. Servant leadership is:

» The differentiator because we answered the question, "Why should we serve others?" We do so because people want to be outstanding performers and high producers. We reviewed and evaluated generational differences. Leaders take the time to understand and value the differences. We read and unpacked how to add value to people to help them fulfill their full potential.

» Leveraging for the Workplace by offering frontline, mid-level, and senior-level leaders ample opportunities to lead by example, be a role model, develop others, and embrace the concept that "leaders are learners."

» Moving organizations forward, which starts with self-reflection and self-assessment. Then leaders are in a much better position to grow our teams through understanding Together Everyone Achieves More. Now, as the workforce shows up each day to perform, they individually and collectively appreciate how their work aligns with the mission, vision, and core values of the organization overall.

A negative attitude that is developed and governed by a negative heart will hinder positive faith. But positive faith encompasses our positive character, which assures us of being in God's favor and perfect will. Bad character produces a bad attitude, which puts limits on God. It hinders us from knowing God, loving Him, and doing His perfect will. A bad, negative character or attitude renders its victim loveless, trustless, without blessings, and useless. A negative attitude produces confusion, division, anger, and rage, and it brings grief to the Holy Spirit. What is the antidote for bad character or any negative attitude? We must allow God, who is the Great Physician, to work with his loving hands to perform brokenness within us as needed. Once brokenness is complete, God can then build our personality, character, constitution, attitude, and temperament, which will, in turn, affect the words we speak.[1]

God has been able to communicate with our hearts, for He alone and none other knows its true condition. Therefore, I now believe that regardless of the title given to a man, every minister of the gospel must consider himself to be a prime candidate for a new heart. All leaders must stay connected to God, pay close attention to what the Lord is saying, and fast and pray without ceasing, saying, "Lord, speak to my heart." The Lord makes many attempts to get through to our emotions, consciousness, feelings, mind, and flesh using various methods:

» He speaks from heaven above.
» He speaks from within us.
» He speaks through his servants.
» He speaks through Christ.
» He speaks by His Word.
» He speaks by His Spirit.
» He speaks to our hearts.

Mankind has spent billions of dollars learning about the physical human body, this world, the moon, and the stars but has spent very little to learn about man's most precious commodity: the spiritual heart. Just as medical heart specialists spend much of their lives researching the natural heart, so should every spiritual leader fervently seek more information and revelation on the spiritual heart. If spiritual leaders will do this, God will enable them to be spiritual heart specialists capable of effectively ministering to His people. In a perfect world—one in which secular physicians recognized the ultimate truth about the heart—we would see medical doctors from local hospitals sitting in the church pews to learn about the awesome spiritual heart from the teachings of church pastors.

A Change of Heart

The heart is a spiritual system that works to release all that abides within it. It makes plans, holds knowledge and memory, and communes with the mind, soul, and will. When the heart is not totally given to God and broke into His will, it becomes the most dangerous weapon upon the earth. We are governed by what our hearts contain, and there can be no change of life or lifestyle until there is a change of heart.

Leadership with a Servant's Heart is on a mission to create, maintain, and sustain a new generation of leaders. Will you be among them?

Reading Group Questions & Topics for Discussion

1. What did you discover about the heart?

_____

_____

_____

_____

_____

2. Generational differences exist in all organizations and will continue for the foreseeable future. How will you advocate for all employees as a leader?

_____

_____

_____

_____

_____

3. Do you assume that introverts are disengaged and disinterested? Why or why not?

_____

_____

_____

_____

_____

4. Helping employees to tap into their potential is an ongoing and recurring process that takes patience. List at least one step that you will take to offer help as needed.

_____

_____

_____

_____

_____

5. As a leader, what are some ways that you can examine your heart?

_____

_____

_____

_____

_____

6. Second Timothy 3:16–17 is quite descriptive as Paul shares with Timothy in preparation for his assignment as a pastor. How does this scripture speak to you?

_____

_____

_____

_____

_____

7. There are several quotes by several prominent leaders that are used in this book. List two that are particularly meaningful to you and why.

_____

_____

_____

_____

_____

8. Do you assume that extroverts are "know-it-alls"? Why or why not?

_____

_____

_____

_____

_____

9. Care, value, honor, empathy, compassion, and respect are words that describe a servant leader. Which description resonates with you the most?

_____

_____

_____

_____

_____

10. In your own words, what does "leading in your workplace" mean to you?

_____

_____

_____

_____

_____

[1] *Code Blue: Serious Matters of the Heart*, by Bishop Dr. Donald R. Downing, Destiny Image Publishers, 2004, pages 54, 92, 107, 112, 117, and 140.

Selected Bibliography & Recommended Reading

101 Important Words about Jesus & the Remarkable Difference They Make, by Len Woods, Our Daily Bread Publishing, 2021.

Code Blue: Serious Matters of the Heart, by Bishop Donald R. Downing, Jr., Destiny Image Publishers, Inc., 2004.

Code Red: Wars of the Heart, by Dr. Donald Downing, Xulon Press, 2005.

Dare to Lead: Brave Work, Tough Conversations, Whole Hearts: Daring Greatly and Rising Strong at Work, by Brene Brown, Ph. D., LMSW, Random House, 2018.

Didn't See It Coming: Overcoming the 7 Greatest Challenges That No One Expects and Everyone Experiences, by Carey Nieuwhof, Waterbrook, 2018.

Empowering Yourself: The Organizational Game Revealed, Second Edition, by Harvey J. Coleman, Author House, 2010.

End Game: The Church's Strategic Move to Save Faith and Family in America, by John Van Epp, Ph. D. and J. P. DeGance, Printing and Graphics Association Mid Atlantic, 2021.

Finding Your Edge: Success Secrets from Top 16 Business Thinkers, by Denise O'Neill, 2019.

Forgiveness: Discover the Power and Reality of Authentic Christian Forgiveness, by Gary Inrig, Our Daily Bread Publishing, 2021.

Fortune Magazine, "GOD and Business: The Surprising Quest for Spiritual Renewal in the American Workplace," by Marc Gunther, 2001.

Good to Great: Why Some Companies Make the Leap...and Others Don't, by Jim Collins, Harper Business, 2001.

How to Lead: Wisdom from the World's Greatest CEOs, Founders, and Game Changers, by David M. Rubenstein, Simon & Schuster, 2020.

Identity Leadership: To Lead Others You Must First Lead Yourself, by Stedman Graham, Center Street, 2019.

Invent & Wander: The Collected Writings of Jeff Bezos, by Jeff Bezos, Harvard Business Review Press & Public Affairs, 2021.

It's Business, Not Social™: Standout, by Colleen McKenna, 2021.

Leader by Accident: Lessons in Leadership, Loss and Life, by Jim Rafferty, Morgan James Publishing with Habitat for Humanity, 2022.

Leaders That Last: How Covenant Friendships Can Help Pastors Thrive, by Gary D. Kinnaman and Alfred H. Ells, Baker Books, 2003.

On Target Living: Your Guide to a Life of Balance, Energy and Vitality, by Chris Johnson, Wiley, 2013.

Playing to Win: How Strategy Really Works, by A. G. Lagley and Roger L. Martin, Harvard Business Review Press, 2013.

Principle-Centered Leadership, by Dr. Stephen R. Covey, Simon and Shuster, 1992.

Thanks for the Feedback: The Science and Art of Receiving Feedback Well, by Douglas Stone and Sheila Heen, Penguin Books, 2014.

The 108 Skills of Natural Born Leaders, by Warren Blank, AMACOM, 2001.

The Coaching Habit: Say Less, As More & Change the Way You Lead Forever, by Michael Bungay Stanier, Box of Crayons Press, 2016.

The DILBERT Future: Thriving on Stupidity in the 21st Century, by Scott Adams, Harper Business, 1997.

The Extraordinary Leader: Turning Good Managers into Great Leaders, by John H. Zenger and Joseph Folkman, McGraw-Hill, 2002.

The Heart of a Leader: Insights on the Art of Influence, by Ken Blanchard, Honor Books, 1999.

The Leadership Wisdom of Solomon: 28 Essential Strategies for Leading with Integrity, by Pat Williams, Standard Publishing, 2010.

The Outward Mindset: Seeing Beyond Ourselves, by The Arbinger Institute, Berrett-Koehler Publishers, Inc., 2016.

The Power of Choice: Embracing Efficacy to Drive Your Career, by Michael C. Hyter, Wiley, 2021.

The Referable Speaker, by Michael Port and Andrew Davis, thereferablespeaker.com, 2021.

U.S. News & World Report, America's Best Leaders: How These Unique Men and Women Are Changing the World, October 30, 2006.

U.S. News & World Report, Special Collector's Edition, American Ingenuity: The Culture of Creativity That Made a Nation Great, 2003.

What Makes Humans Tick? Exploring the Best Validated Assessments, by Brandon Parker, Jennifer Larsen, MAED, MSP, MBA, and Tony Alessandra, Ph. D., Indie Books International, 2021.

Work Disrupted: Opportunity, Resilience, and Growth in the Accelerated Future of Work, by Jeff Schwartz, Wiley, 2021.

Workforce 2000: Work and Workers for the 21st Century, Executive Summary, by William B. Johnston and Arnold E. Packer, Hudson Institute Inc., 1987.

Working from Home: Everything You Need to Know About Living and Working Under the Same Roof, by Paul and Sarah Edwards, AT&T, Jeremy P. Tarcher, Inc., 1990.

About the Author

Because, he says, "God uses ordinary people to accomplish extraordinary things," Kevin Wayne Johnson has taken up the task of developing individual and organizational operating excellence as his life's ministry. He trains, mentors, and coaches in order to coax audiences to live out their gifts and, in the words of his national best-selling book series, to then "Give God the Glory!" This series of eight books has earned the current radio and former television co-host some 19 literary awards since 2001. Gayle King, an editor-at-large for *O, The Oprah Magazine*, praised his work, writing to him that "Your book, Kevin, touched me."

Johnson is the founder & CEO of the Johnson Leadership Group, LLC, and an independent certified coach, trainer, mentor, and speaker with the internationally recognized John Maxwell Team, where he leads learning experiences that are tailored to meet the specific needs of the audience to help maximize efficiency, growth, awareness, and effectiveness. He provides organizations, and the people who work within them, with the tools to forge effective personal and interpersonal

communication and delivers training on the elements of dynamic relationships to equip teams with the attitudes and attributes needed to develop individuals into leaders. He does so through motivating workshops, seminars, insightful keynote speeches, and compassion-ate coaching—all to encourage personal and professional growth.

Johnson enjoyed a thirty-four-year career in government and private industry as a frontline, mid-level, and senior-level leader. He led workforce development, training, organizational change, acquisition/procurement, customer service, client relationships, budget, security, records management, property administration, facilities, and human resources organizations during his tenure. He was a key leader on the National Performance Review for Procurement and Customer Service Reform under the first Clinton Administration, has testified before the U.S. House of Representatives Small Business Committee on Procurement Reform, and wrote testimony that was presented before the District of Columbia's Committee for Government Operations.

A native of Richmond, Virginia, Johnson earned a B.S. in Business Administration and Management from Virginia Commonwealth University's School of Business and completed course work toward an M.B.A. at both Marymount University and the University of Colorado at Colorado Springs. He earned the Master's Certification in Government Contracting from the George Washington University, Washington, DC.

He is an ordained Church of God Ministries, Inc. (Anderson, Indiana) minister and has served in a myriad of leadership positions over the past twenty-two years in the local church, to include senior pastor, as well as regionally, nationally, and internationally in Kenya, St. Lucia, Turks and Caicos, and London. His latest book— *Leadership with a Servant's Heart: Leading through Personal*

Relationships ©2019—is an Amazon.com new release best-seller in two categories and earned nine literary awards in 2020 and 2021. Johnson is currently serving a four-year team as Faith Community Commissioner for Suicide Prevention under Maryland Governor Larry Hogan.

He lives in Clarksville, Maryland, with his wife of twenty-nine years, Gail, and raised three sons. He has one goddaughter and two god-granddaughters.

Kevin Wayne Johnson is a proud certified member, speaker, coach, mentor, and trainer with the nationally recognized John Maxwell Team. Maxwell has been universally recognized as the number one leadership expert for many, many years.

To learn more about Kevin's profile with the John Maxwell Team, go here: www.johncmaxwellgroup.com/kevinjohnson.

Listen to Kevin Wayne Johnson on the Words of Wisdom (WOW) Champion Podcast. It is produced and distributed by Elite Conversations Media, twice monthly. Kevin shares insightful strategies, tools, tips, nuggets, and principles that will heighten your level of awareness on the timely topic of servant leadership.

For more information, go to:

https://www.eliteconversations.com/mypodcast.html

Leadership with a Servant's Heart: *Leading through Personal Relationships* ©2019 earned nine literary awards in 2020 and 2021.

To order your copy, visit:

www.thejohnsonleadershipgroup.com/leadership-book

OR

www.amazon.com

OR

Mail a check or money order to:

Writing for the Lord Ministries
6400 Shannon Court
Clarksville, MD 21029 USA

Total price to include shipping & handling: $28.00

Listen to co-host Kevin Wayne Johnson on the monthly radio show at www.blogtalkradio.com/christianauthorsontour, alongside the Founder and Director of Christian Authors on Tour, Lynn Pinder. This monthly radio show has aired since 2009. To join us every first Friday at 2:00 p.m. EST, dial in here:

563-999-3025.

CPSIA information can be obtained
at www.ICGtesting.com
Printed in the USA
LVHW050442231022
731282LV00001B/6

9 780988 303867